Developing and Managing Community Water Supplies

Jan Davis and Gerry Garvey,
with Michael Wood

Development Guidelines No. 8

Oxfam
UK and Ireland

A catalogue record for this book is available from the British Library

ISBN 0 85598 192 X Hardback
ISBN 0 85598 193 8 Paperback

Cover Photo: A community water supply in Ethiopia (Gerry Garvey/Oxfam)

Other titles in the Oxfam Development Guidelines series:

Published by Oxfam, 274 Banbury Road, Oxford OX2 7DZ
Designed and typeset by Oxfam Design Unit (NY284/PK/93)
Printed in Great Britain at The Alden Press, Oxford
on environmentally-friendly paper
Set in 9.5/12pt Garamond

Contents

Preface

This book aims to pass on field experience and the lessons learned from community water supply programmes in Africa. Most of the experience comes from programmes implemented in Ethiopia and Ghana between 1986-92. The intention is to present an overview of the development and management of community water supplies to provide guidance for future water supply programmes. The aim is to bridge the gap between theory and practice and to integrate social and technical issues.

The book has been written for programme managers and senior extension and technical staff of community groups, external support agencies, in particular, non-governmental organisations (NGOs), and government agencies supporting community water supply programmes. The book provides guidelines for:

- planning and managing fieldwork;
- training community members and programme staff;
- preparing programme proposals.

The book is divided into two parts:

Part One looks at the links between water and health, and the importance of hygiene education in maximising potential health benefits. The roles of different individuals within communities and agencies, and their views concerning water supplies, are considered.

Part Two looks at the development of community water supplies from the viewpoint of the 'programme cycle'. The sequence of planning, preparing a proposal, implementing a programme of projects, and managing improved water supplies is considered in detail.

There are numerous short case studies illustrating the practical issues faced in the field. Most of the case studies are taken from non-governmental organisation experience, though the viewpoints of government agencies, those involved in foreign government aid-programmes, church organisations, and community groups are also included. The majority of the case studies are based on the authors' direct experience whilst working with Oxfam, the Ethiopian Water Supply and Sewerage Authority, the Ethiopian Water Works Construction Authority, the Ghana Water and Sewerage Corporation, and the Canadian International Development Agency.

The guidelines set out in this book could be used by programme managers in staff training. The case study approach brings to life some of the issues considered and the cases themselves are intended to act as starting points for further group discussion as part of a training programme. The case studies should be supplemented by examples from people's own experience.

Whether used in training or for reference, it is hoped that the issues considered and the guidelines presented will be of interest and value to a wide range of people involved in developing and managing community water supplies.

Acknowledgements

Thanks are due to the many individuals who gave their time to review the drafts and provide valuable contributions: Astier Almedon, Nega Bazezew, Richard Carter, John Dindiok, Ben Fawcett, Peter Howsam, Nick King, Paul Smith-Lomas, Chris Mason, Mona Mehta, Joy Morgan, Adelina Mwau, Magdalena Barros Nock, Ben Pugansoa, Diane Sutton, Alan Reed, Catherine Robinson, James Tumwine, and Bridget Walker.

Thanks are also due to Maria Arzayus, who provided valuable administrative back-up in Oxford, and to Anni Fjord for her patience and support during the intensive periods of writing in Denmark, and to Laerke and Lars for providing us with so many distractions.

Jan Davis
Gerry Garvey
Michael Wood
July 1993

Introduction

This book considers the development and management of community water supplies through the partnership of the community and a support agency.

What is meant by the term 'agency'?

In this book, the word 'agency' is used to refer to a range of 'implementing agencies' which include: national and international non-governmental organisations (NGOs), church organisations, bi-lateral and multi-lateral aid agencies, and government departments responsible for water. Where reference is made to 'funding agencies' the word 'donor' will be used. Some organisations both implement and fund programmes, and these will be referred to as 'agencies'.

What is meant by a 'community water supply'?

To answer this question, three alternative approaches to the development of a community water supply will be considered:

1 Agency developed — Agency managed

This approach is similar to that of a government water agency which develops a supply, then operates and maintains it for a community. The community may, or may not, pay for the service, depending on government policy. The members of the community do not participate in the construction and management of the supply. Their only involvement is as consumers of the water.

2 Agency/Community developed — Agency/Community managed

The agency and community work together to develop a supply. This might, for example, be an NGO programme in which 'community participation' is encouraged. Operation and maintenance may be shared between the NGO and the community for as long as the NGO is able to continue its support.

3 Community developed — Community managed

This is the most common situation, in which communities develop and manage their own supplies, such as traditional water holes, dug wells and springs, without any external support.

Each of these three approaches may have its own problems. The first approach may provide an adequate water supply but only for as long as the water agency can operate and maintain the system. If the agency in the second approach withdraws its support, the community may not be in a position to manage the system on its own in the long term. In the third approach, many of the sources may not provide enough water; they may be polluted, and far from the village; and it may be difficult to get water at certain times of the year.

Obviously, the reason for starting many water supply programmes is to overcome the problems associated with the third type of water provision. However, in trying to solve one set of problems, new problems of long-term operation and maintenance may be encountered. If, as commonly happens, improved supplies fail because of poor operation and maintenance, communities return to their former inadequate sources.

Governments often have problems in managing water supplies, especially in rural areas, because they lack resources. Unless there is reliable long-term external support, it is necessary to develop water supplies which communities can largely manage themselves. This means looking very carefully at the balance of responsibilities between community and agency.

Reducing community dependence on external support

If communities can take a greater share of the responsibility for managing water supplies, they will be less dependent on external support. In some situations the dependency may be eliminated altogether. The title of this book is intended to stress the fact that developing and managing community water supplies go together. A supply cannot be managed successfully if the development stage does not prepare a community for regular management tasks. Therefore, the steps towards community management begin at the initial planning stage of a project and continue through to the final completion and management of the supply by the community.

Adequate preliminary planning of a programme is important for both successful implementation and for long-term community management. For this reason, the planning stage has been thoroughly covered in this book.

In reality, many improved supplies still require final technical back-up from an external body, even if the regular operation and maintenance can be managed by communities themselves. Communities and support agencies must consider how this back-up can be provided if supplies are to be sustained.

The need for a flexible approach

The principle that agencies should support communities to develop and manage their own water supplies may be easier to state than to put into practice. Circumstances, and the nature of each community, will require a flexible approach in each situation. The following two case studies illustrate the contrasting circumstances in which water programmes in Ethiopia and Ghana have recently developed. They show very different relationships between the community and agency:

A water development programme in Wollo Province, northern Ethiopia, evolved out of an emergency water programme for displaced people in feeding centres during the Ethiopian famine of 1983/85. The political environment in Wollo was extremely tense due to the proximity of civil war in neighbouring Tigray Province. The combination of famine and conflict destroyed many traditional community structures, enabling government control of the population to be strengthened through politically-appointed community representatives. In such a situation, community development was highly centralised and consultation with individual community members became very difficult, if not impossible. Over time, the programme evolved methods of consultation which allowed some degree of community participation and decision making, though within the political constraints of an authoritarian centralised government. Unfortunately, the expansion of civil war into Wollo in 1989 forced the closure of the programme.

In contrast, a programme in the Northern Region of Ghana, originated through an already close contact between a community and an NGO:

The NGO was funding an animal-traction project to train farmers to plough with bullocks. The training took place towards the end of the dry season in readiness for the rains when farmland would be prepared for planting. This was a very hot, dry time and water was scarce. It was difficult to obtain enough water for either people or cattle, and this led the community to discuss the water problem with the NGO. This was the beginning of a new water programme.

The Ethiopian and Ghanaian programmes have different political and cultural backgrounds. Each offers its own challenges and demonstrates practical limitations as to how agencies can effectively support communities in developing and managing their own water supplies. These practical limitations, and the ways around them, are considered in this book.

The scale of programmes

NGOs work on a much smaller scale than government agencies or large multilateral aid agencies. NGOs tend to focus their activities at local level, and associate themselves with identifiable community groups. The approach of large support agencies tends to be to work with government agencies at a regional or national level.

The approaches of the different agencies complement each other. Planning at a regional level provides the framework for the support of activities at the community level. Support at the community level provides the experience and feedback necessary for the successful planning of regional programmes.

NGOs can develop approaches with communities which work at the household level, as in the following case:

Health promoters in northern Ghana arranged informal meetings in extended-family compounds. The relaxed setting encouraged questions, especially from women, and general participation, which would not have been possible in a large village meeting.

But how many people can be contacted and educated in this way? For a small NGO programme supporting a specific community this approach may be effective and appropriate. But would it be possible to scale up such an approach to operate regionally? How would all the health promoters be recruited and trained? Where would the considerable funds required come from? A larger-scale approach may be possible, but at a cost which might not be sustainable in the long term. Therefore, what may be appropriate and possible on a small scale may not be realistic when scaled up. When considering the stages of a programme, therefore, it is necessary to have in mind the scale of the programme and the different approaches for the various levels within it.

In practice, most agencies work at two levels:

• at the community level, supporting community initiative, learning from the community, and building on existing practice;

• at the overall programme level, adopting an approach which allows for the development of structures to support community initiatives.

A catalyst for change

A water programme has the potential to act as a catalyst for change. The process of organising the implementation of water projects and long-term management of water supplies can be a starting point from which further development initiatives might flow.

The collection and use of water is predominantly in the hands of women. A water programme, therefore, provides an opportunity for women to be centrally involved in the development process — if they are allowed to be. It can be an opportunity for women to strengthen their often weak position in decision making and control of resources. The central role of women in water supply, hygiene, and sanitation has been emphasised throughout the book, just as it should be in practice.

Water supply technologies

The water supply technologies referred to in the case studies tend to be hand-dug wells and protected springs. This is because of the specific programmes from which the case studies have been taken. It is not intended to give the impression that hand-dug wells and protected springs are the preferred technologies in every situation, but rather to use the case studies to highlight issues which are generally applicable to a broad range of technologies.

Water supply in different communities

Most of the case studies are taken from rural water supply programmes. Nevertheless, the underlying principles which apply to rural supplies are also appropriate to a broader range of community water supplies in urban, peri-urban and refugee communities.

The integrated approach

Water programmes are generally intended to improve the health, social, and economic conditions of individuals within communities. However, if water programmes are to have an impact on health they cannot stand alone, designed only to improve water supplies. An integrated approach is needed which considers a range of concerns — water, sanitation, hygiene education, and environmental protection. As this approach is crucial to maximising the potential benefits of a water programme, the various factors involved are considered first, in Chapter 1.

PART 1

Issues in community water supply

1

Water and environmental health

This chapter introduces the range of factors which need to be considered in the development of a community water supply.

1.1 Why develop water supplies?

There may be a combination of reasons for developing a community water supply, but these can be divided into two broad categories:

- to improve social and economic conditions;
- to improve the health of the community.

Social and economic benefits

The social conditions which could be improved by the development of a community water supply include a reduction in the effort and time required to collect water. This could reduce the workload of women, which is often very heavy, as they are usually the collectors of water. In this case, the aim of the programme would be to bring the collection point closer to the women's homes, in other words, to improve the *availability* of water. This might be achieved by digging wells in the village itself or piping water from a distant spring.

Improving the availability of water may have economic benefits as well as social benefits. Increasing the quantity of water that is available and bringing the water closer to the point of use can help productive activities such as crop washing and processing, small-scale gardening, the dyeing of cloth, and other income-generating activities.

Health benefits

The majority of infectious diseases in developing countries are related to water in some way. Water-related diseases include those which are carried by water or where water provides the vital link in their transmission. They also include diseases which can be prevented or reduced by the hygienic handling and use of water.

Disease transmission commonly occurs as a result of the unhygienic disposal of human and household waste combined with poor hygienic practices. Water can be safe at a source but may become contaminated during collection, carrying, handling and use. Hygiene improvements often depend on having an adequate quantity of water for washing, regardless of its quality. Therefore, the provision of safe water is not in itself sufficient to guarantee an improvement in the health of a community.

Improvements in health will only be achieved by an integrated approach which includes, in addition to safe water supplies, effective sanitation and an emphasis on good hygiene practices through complementary hygiene promotion activities.

An assessment of the health problems of a community can be carried out in the early stages of a programme through a preliminary health survey. The health survey results will help to compare the relative importance of water supply and sanitation improvements, the promotion of good hygiene practices, and other primary health care activities. Many agencies will not have sufficient funds to support a full range of integrated activities. A preliminary assessment, therefore, can help to identify the most important environmental health activities on which limited funds can best be spent.

The following sections will briefly introduce some important issues concerning the safe disposal of human waste, and people's hygiene behaviour.

1.2 Sanitation

Where there is no improved form of sanitation, many people practice what has been called 'open-field' defaecation. Custom may dictate location and the areas which men and women use. Children may defaecate in or near the household yard. Some of these traditional sanitation practices are uncontrolled and can pose serious health risks. Improved sanitation aims to contain and safely dispose of human excreta.

Improvements to sanitation may be approached at a community or individual household level. Community sanitation — in the form of public latrines — is usually found in more densely-populated areas, in towns, where a lack of space makes it difficult to build many individual latrines. There are, however, problems in managing community latrines, and in rural areas, where space is normally not a problem, improved sanitation is often encouraged at the individual household level. `

When planning an integrated programme of water supply and sanitation activities, it is necessary to adopt different approaches to the two components. This is because:

- Improvements to a water supply generally attract more immediate support than improvements to sanitation, because the benefits are more obvious.

- As a consequence of this, the time required to generate interest in improved household sanitation is generally longer than the time required to generate interest in an improved water supply.

- Some households will be better able to afford improvements to their sanitation than other households. In contrast, the cost of improving a water supply can be spread evenly throughout a community.

These points of difference between the development of an improved water supply and the development of improved sanitation mean that each will require a different approach. The emphasis of a sanitation programme is on education, to change people's behaviour and to stimulate demand for improved sanitation facilities. The same kind of stimulation of interest may not be necessary in the case of an improved water supply, where the emphasis will be on construction, better use of the water, and the development of effective community management.

The cost of improved sanitation may be a problem. Even if households are interested in improving their sanitation, the cost of building latrines may be more than they can afford:

In the village of Zezencho, in the Gurage region of Ethiopia, model pit-latrines constructed using concrete slabs cost about 200 birr ($US40). People could not afford this, so an alternative design of latrine was adopted using local materials. It consisted of a pit covered with cedar logs, across which were laid bamboo poles lashed together with eucalyptus rope and then plastered with clay. The cost of this model was about 60 birr ($12). Most people could afford this sum.

Latrines will only be built *and used* if households are convinced of their benefits and they can afford to build them.

Eastern Sudan. A
ventilated improved pit
latrine slab and vent
pipe before the
surrounding screen was
built.

Jan Davis/Oxfam

An integrated approach to improving health

The different components of water supply and sanitation, supported by
hygiene education, within an integrated programme, may have different
time scales and require personnel with different skills. A sanitation
component, therefore, cannot just be 'added-on' to a water supply
programme without careful consideration of the implications.

It is not the intention of this section, or this book, to go into detail
concerning the approaches to improving sanitation, or the sanitation
methods which might be encouraged. However, as part of an integrated
approach to the improvement of people's health, it is important to
recognise the need to improve sanitation alongside improvements to

water supplies. Both components of sanitation and water supply need the support of a programme of hygiene education designed to promote good hygiene behaviour.

The links between sanitation, water supply, and the promotion of good hygiene practices through hygiene education will be made at appropriate points throughout the book. Information on approaches to improved sanitation and hygiene promotion will be found in the references given at the end of each relevant chapter.

1.3 Hygiene behaviour

Many health problems are due to poor hygiene behaviour. Health-related water programmes, therefore, should consider carefully the changes in hygiene practices needed to complement improved water and sanitation facilities. The case studies in this section illustrate the different aspects of hygiene behaviour that must be considered.

Gerry Garvey/Oxfam

Boditi, Ethiopia. Good personal hygiene includes hand washing.

13

Personal hygiene

Many water-related diseases are transmitted through inadequate body and hand washing. Regular washing can reduce the chance of contracting skin and eye diseases. Washing hands after defaecation can reduce the transmission of micro-organisms which cause diarrhoea:

> *A water programme health-survey in West Mamprusi District, Ghana, indicated that diarrhoea, infected eyes, and scabies were common. These diseases were connected with poor personal hygiene, and inadequate body washing, especially of the hands.*
>
> *An objective of the programme, therefore, was to integrate measures designed to increase the amount of water available for washing, with education on the benefits of regular body and hand washing.*

Household hygiene

Improvements to existing methods of water handling and of its use in the home could make a big difference to people's health. In order to identify poor hygiene behaviour, the following questions might be asked:

- Is water stored in a hygienic way?

- Are collection and storage containers regularly cleaned?

- Are containers covered?

- Is a distinction made between water for drinking and water for other uses?

- Is water handled safely in the home?

- Is there any kind of household water-treatment and is it hygienic?

Storage of water in the home is a form of treatment, and a reserve in times of failed supply:

> *The improved Kubore village well only provided enough safe water for drinking needs. Water for washing and cooking still had to be collected from the old contaminated source. So households allocated different pots for the storage of the two types of water.*

There are often constraints on storage owing to the cost of containers. A programme may be able to influence this situation by considering storage options, and the production and availability of containers.

Allowing water to settle overnight in a storage pot can improve water quality. The clear water then needs to be poured into a clean pot, and the sediment in the first pot cleaned out. There are a range of substances which can be used to help to speed up the process of settlement:

Settlement is more rapid if suspended particles can be encouraged to join together, so making them heavier. Powdered alum is the chemical used in many water-treatment works to help the rapid settlement of solids. In parts of West Africa 'alum' rock can be purchased in local markets. A small amount is dissolved by stirring the rock in a water pot for a few minutes. The alum collects the particles together and the solids settle to the bottom of the pot.

Different societies use a variety of substances to help the settlement of water. Pots must be regularly cleaned after the settlement of the solids.

Community hygiene

Water from an improved supply may be safe but can become contaminated during collection and carrying:

The source of water in a refugee settlement in Eastern Sudan was from a borehole fitted with an electric submersible pump. Water was pumped to an overhead tank which supplied tapstands in a central water-yard. The quality of the water was tested at the taps and found to be very good. Further tests were then carried out on water samples from household pots. The quality of water was found to have significantly decreased.

Water was transported from the tapstands to the household pots in large rubber bags carried on donkeys. Short plastic pipes trailed from the taps to fill the bags. When not in use, the pipes would hang from the taps and rub against the donkeys, and even fall on the ground. The pipes, therefore, contaminated the water when the bags were filled.

Communal water points need to be kept in a sanitary condition and used hygienically if health benefits are to follow from the safe water supplied.

The recognition of existing poor hygiene behaviour is a first step in developing hygiene education aimed at reducing water- and sanitation-related diseases in a particular community. It should be the aim of hygiene education to encourage a community's interest in improvements to water supplies and sanitation through a greater understanding of why improvements are necessary. A community which accepts agency support without a clear understanding of the intended benefits may not be in a position to make full use of the improvements. A community which requests assistance for the improvement of its water supply and sanitation facilities, based on a clear understanding of why they are necessary, is going to be well motivated to look after the improved services and use them effectively.

1.4 Environmental factors

Land use, pollution, and changes in the weather are among the environmental factors which can affect water sources and which need to be considered when developing supplies.

Land use can have an important effect on the functioning of small-scale reservoirs:

Some 'dug-outs', or small reservoirs, in northern Ghana silted up in a short period of time. This was because of the farming of the land from

Wolayta, Ethiopia. Measuring the water depth in a well can be made easy.

Gerry Garvey/Oxfam

which the runoff water was collected. The loose, cultivated soils were easily swept into the dug-outs by the runoff water. This silt-laden water caused reductions in the capacity of the reservoir. The result was that the dug-outs could no longer store enough water for the dry season.

Control of the use of land near water sources such as reservoirs can help to protect them from damage and pollution.

It is advisable to have a means of monitoring critical changes in the environment. For example, it is important to include a means of measuring changes in water level in sealed wells with pumps:

Covered wells fitted with handpumps in Wolayta, Ethiopia, had been drying without warning. A means of quickly monitoring the level of water in each well, without disturbing the well cover or pump, was required. A small diameter galvanised iron pipe was cast into each well cover slab. The upper end of the pipe was fitted with a cap, to be unscrewed by a technician using a pipe wrench. This allowed a water-level tape, or a weight on a length of string, to be lowered through the pipe. The water level could then be easily measured in just a few minutes.

Small-scale community programmes can make useful contributions to regional or national data bases by sharing information such as groundwater levels and rainfall records. The long-term monitoring of groundwater levels is important:

In the Upper Regions of Ghana, the Ghana Water and Sewerage Corporation has been monitoring the fluctuations in groundwater levels for many years. Every six months the static water level at selected handpump sites is measured: at the end of the dry season and at the end of the wet season. In 1987 the results showed that after ten years the water table had dropped an average of three metres across the region.

Data of this kind can be used to determine the depth of future wells and boreholes, and the safety margin to use when installing rising mains for handpumps. This ensures that they do not dry up prematurely, so that sources can be used throughout the year.

Sources may go dry because of increased use of water for irrigation. As wells are dug, or drilled, and farmers are able to afford powered pumps for irrigation, the amount of water taken from the ground can be so great that it significantly lowers the groundwater table. This has happened in several countries, especially in parts of Asia where powered pumping has increased following improved economic conditions. The result has been that domestic wells have dried up. Wells must then be deepened, or the amount of water which farmers are allowed to pump from the ground controlled.

In some countries the water table has been dropping dramatically, owing to reduced rainfall and rapid run-off caused by deforestation and poor farming practices:

In Eritrea, efforts are being made to replenish groundwater supplies by building small dams across narrow valleys. This creates a body of water which can be used for domestic purposes or for irrigating gardens. It also serves to maintain the level of the water table in the area, so that nearby wells will not dry up during periods of drought.

Water quality can be affected by pollution upstream and by underground infiltration of pollutants:

A heavily used, but unprotected, spring in Matuga, Uganda, flowed from near the bottom of a small hill. On inspection of the site a septic tank was found serving a large house only 30 metres up the hill. Since the spring was a main source of water for the village, the authorities ordered the closure of the septic tank and a check on the quality of the spring water.

Wells and springs are open to contamination from pit latrines, septic tanks, and other waste disposal sites. Polluted water can travel long distances underground when conditions allow. Not only fractures in rock but laterite soils, commonly found in tropical climates, can allow the 'piping' of water over significant distances. The safe distance between a latrine and source therefore depends on the soil conditions.

The development and use of water supplies can, in turn, have an effect on the local environment:

Overgrazing around the water-yards of Eastern Sudan was clear to see. Each borehole water-supply attracted herds of camel, sheep and goats, which consumed grass, and permanently damaged shrubs and leafy trees in an area radiating out from each water-yard.

This example illustrates the importance of considering the environmental consequences of actions to improve water supplies. Measures need to be taken to prevent such adverse effects. This involves close consultation with users. In the above case, consultation with herd owners was necessary to discuss the control of animal grazing around water-yards.

The watering of cattle from a drinking-water source can cause a major environmental health problem, as this case from Damot Gale, Wolayta, Ethiopia, shows:

The issue of cattle watering was raised at a general community meeting. The existing well had no cattle trough, so every day there was a fight between women trying to collect water from the handpump, and men trying to water their cattle, also using the handpump. The surrounding area soon became very muddy, with pools of stagnant water ponding around the well. These pools became ideal breeding-grounds for mosquitoes.

Bolosso, Ethiopia. A badly-protected spring with poor drainage.

During discussion with an agency extension agent, it was decided to construct a drainage channel leading to a cattle trough. This had the effect of separating drinking-water collection from cattle watering. An agreement on times during the day when the handpump could be used to supply drinking water and when it could be used for cattle watering was also reached. The handpump caretaker was responsible for regulating these times.

Drainage from improved supplies, such as springs and wells, and

19

household wastewater drainage, can create localised environmental problems. The review of a spring-protection programme in Bolosso District, Wolayta, Ethiopia, resulted in the following comments on the spring drainage:

'Many sites are a sea of mud, in which women have to walk knee-deep to collect water from the spring box outlet pipe. The main aim of spring protection is to protect the quality of the water at source and make it convenient to collect. It is a pity that both these aims are at risk because of the possibility of re-contaminating the spring water and making it inconvenient to collect because of the very bad drainage.'

The review was followed by a remedial programme to improve drainage at all the protected springs.

Both the environmental effects of improving water supplies and the effects of the environment on water sources must be taken into account when developing community water supplies.

1.5 Aims and benefits

The activities of a programme will vary according to the desired aims and benefits. Social and economic aims will concentrate on:

- improving access to water;

- increasing the quantity of available water.

Health aims will concentrate on a combination of:

- increasing the quantity of available water;

- improving water quality;

- changing hygiene behaviour;

- improving sanitation.

Achieving one aim may fulfil another. They are often complementary:

In the foothills of Mount Kenya, the communities of Murugi-Mugomango pipe water from a mountain stream to consumers who each have a yard tap. The water consumed has an important economic value. It is used to irrigate small gardens and for crop processing, especially coffee washing. People pay regularly on a monthly basis, and the system is well-maintained as a result.

The piped water has a clear economic value but there is also an improvement in social conditions for the women who, before the piped supply was in place, had to walk long distances for water.

An external support agency might want to assist in the improvement of a water supply in order to improve the health of a community. Community members, however, might have other reasons for wanting to improve a supply:

One of the diggers at a well-construction site in Kubagna, northern Ghana, disputed the fact that guinea-worm disease was transmitted through contaminated water. He said this could not be the case because for many years other members of his family had suffered from guinea-worm but he had never had it. He commented, 'How can you blame the water when we all drink from the same pot?'

The man was keen to dig the well. However, his reasons for being enthusiastic were not connected with risks to his health. Many people in the village felt the same way. They were more concerned to have a water source nearby, instead of having to walk many kilometres to collect water at the height of the dry season. In this, and other cases, success in achieving one benefit can be used to achieve others.

But a word of warning! In some cases, so called improvements to existing water sources can lead to a worse situation. Unfortunately, there are many cases which illustrate this point: from the spring which dried up after it was protected, to the supply with poor drainage which encouraged mosquito breeding. This case study from Ethiopia shows the problems that can arise when a community cannot carry out maintenance:

A traditional well near Hayk, in Wollo, Ethiopia, was protected and a handpump installed. Some months later the pump broke down but it could not be repaired for a long time because of the lack of spare parts. With no alternative access to the well water, women had to walk even further than they had before the 'improvement'. They wished the traditional source had never been interfered with.

An alternative access to the well water could have been provided so that when the pump broke down water could still be drawn by rope and bucket. One of the most important roles of an agency is to provide good technical support to the community. This is a serious responsibility, and includes the development of supplies which can be maintained by the community when external agency support is withdrawn.

Some of the aims and benefits of a water supply programme will now be considered.

Northern Ghana. Water is carried in 30 to 35 litre steel drums on the head.

Reducing carrying distances and improving access to sources

Reducing carrying distances can shorten women's working hours and have significant physical benefits for water collectors. There are many problems related to carrying water. One of the most common methods of transporting water is on the head. Water containers can be clay pots, gourds, plastic buckets, drums, jerry cans, and so on:

> *In Ghana, women use round drums made from recycled sheet steel to carry water. The drums are made in towns and repaired by travelling artisans. Capacities vary from 20 to 30 litres. A young child will accompany her mother to the source and carry water in a small calabash until she graduates to a five-litre bowl and later a small steel drum. Women will sometimes walk for over an hour with these 30kg weights on their heads.*

The burden of water carrying

Women can suffer deformities, headaches and exhaustion due to the range of heavy carrying work they are required to do. For many low-income women the working day is excessively long. In sub-Saharan Africa, for example, the collection and carrying of water and fuel-wood over considerable distances can result in women having only a few hours' sleep a night in the dry season.

Accidents whilst carrying water can have tragic consequences:

A young woman from the village of Tari, in northern Ghana, stumbled whilst carrying a full container of water. The edge of the heavy steel container fell onto her big toe and cut it off. This tragedy meant that she could no longer balance a load on her head. Women carry everything on their heads; water, items to and from market, and firewood. In her society, no man would marry a woman who could not carry the essential loads of everyday life.

In more mountainous regions it becomes difficult to balance water containers on the head and an alternative is to carry a container on the back. In the highlands of Ethiopia carrying heavy water pots on the back can cause spinal damage:

The container used in the highlands of Ethiopia is a clay pot with a rounded bottom and narrow neck. Water is collected from the source with a gourd and poured into the pot. Clay pots are heavy even before they are filled with water. When full, the pot can weigh from 25 to 35kg. It is carried on the back, resting on the base of the spine, and held with a strap around the shoulders. Regular carrying of water can leave permanent scars where straps have rubbed the skin, and in some cases can result in the deformation of the spine.

Wolayta, Ethiopia. Carrying water by animal can reduce the burden on women.

23

There is no doubt that water carrying is a burden for many women and children. Improving carrying practices, however, is not easy. Any new method of carrying water would have to be acceptable to users, and cheaper and easier to use than their existing methods.

Where new technology is introduced to improve domestic water carrying, such as bicycles or donkey carts, there is the chance that men may become involved. Men may want to control and benefit from the new technology. This may be an advantage to women, as it could reduce their workload; but the disadvantage is that women do not then have access to the new technology. As a consequence, women may lose control over water collection but still be responsible for its use and management in the home.

Access to water sources

Safe physical access to water sources is an important consideration for water users. It may sometimes be difficult, even dangerous, to collect water:

> *The community of Boneya in Wollo, Ethiopia, relied entirely on springs in a series of limestone caves for their drinking-water supply. To collect water, several young women climbed down about ten metres, and formed a human chain from the bottom up to the top of the cave. Water was passed to each woman in a small gourd, and received by older women sitting at the top. This way of collecting water was extremely dangerous and the young women frequently fell and injured themselves.*

Improving access to a physically dangerous source can be a major benefit in itself.

Deciding on who has responsibility for maintaining access to a water source may become a problem:

> *A drainage channel became overgrown with vegetation, and waste water began to pond around a well, in Bolosso, Ethiopia. A group of women using the well said that they could easily clean the channel in a few hours, but that kind of work was traditionally done by men in their part of Ethiopia, so they could not become involved. However, the men were too busy with other matters and the well was not their priority.*

A frequent difficulty with many communal facilities is that each individual will know a problem exists but no one person will be prepared to do anything about it. The solution lies in effective community organisation.

Boneya, Ethiopia.
Difficult and dangerous
access to a source.

Gerry Garvey/Oxfam

Hygienic access to water sources plays an important role in preventing the transmission of disease:

The Village Water Reservoirs Project, Tamale, Ghana, was concerned to prevent people and animals walking into reservoir water intended for human consumption. The reservoirs were fenced. Infiltration pipes were laid from the centre of each reservoir to wells set into the banks. Water for both humans and animals was collected from the wells. The access was conveniently situated by the side of the reservoirs but far enough away to prevent contamination.

Carefully planned access can have a major impact on water quality, in addition to ensuring physical safety in the collection of water.

Increasing water quantity

Adequate quantities of water are required for healthy living: for drinking, cooking and washing. The World Health Organisation recommends that the minimum daily amount of water per person should be 27 litres. Many people, however, manage on far less than 27 litres a day. The quantity of water people use is partly related to how much is conveniently available:

A survey during the dry season in the community of Guwa Meda in Wollo, Ethiopia showed that water collectors, on average, collected only five litres of water per day for each person in their household. They spent about 30 minutes walking to and from their water source, a protected spring. Additional time was spent queuing at the source because most people preferred to collect water at a particular time, either early in the morning or late in the afternoon, rather than throughout the day.

If water sources are at a long distance from the village, this can significantly restrict the amount of water it is possible to carry home. In such a situation, a primary objective of a water programme is to develop sources, or pipe water, closer to the point of use.

However, it does not automatically follow that having easy access to a water supply will mean that people will use more water:

A survey in the village of Garbota, Sidamo Region, Ethiopia, showed that many households had a shallow well in their compound. But it was discovered that the daily consumption, including washing, was only 15 litres per person.

This highlights yet again the need for education in the use of water. People tend to be healthier if their standards of hygiene are good. Good hygiene depends on using enough water.

Collecting water is only one of several activities women and children have to carry out during the day. They may be restricted to collecting water at certain times of the day, therefore a high demand on a supply can be expected at preferred collection times. A potential problem of wells with insufficient yield is that they can become dry for short periods at these peak collection times. People then have to wait for the well to recharge.

The continued functioning of a water supply depends upon a reliable source and a reliable system of obtaining water from the source. The reliability of a source is often determined by seasonal changes. Some wells and springs may fail towards the end of the dry season owing to a drop in the water table. This is the time when water is needed most but when supplies are least reliable:

Wolayta, Ethiopia. Waiting for a well to recharge will reduce the time available for collecting water and, therefore, the quantity of water used.

A water programme in Wolayta, Ethiopia, conducted a survey of 100 hand dug wells in the dry season. The results showed that 60 of the wells dried up for a period of time during each day causing queuing problems, and five of the wells were completely dry.

Many traditional wells and ponds fail towards the end of the dry season and need improvement if they are to last until the rains. Improved sources can also become dry. At the time of construction the supply may be adequate, but when the population increases, or there is a severe dry period, the source dries up. It is therefore preferable to dig wells or drill boreholes during the dry season when groundwater levels are near their seasonal low-point.

Improving water quality

People may have different ideas about water quality:

A protected open well in Kelkalcha, Wollo, Ethiopia was constructed next to a seasonally-flowing stream. During the dry season, women and children were seen collecting water from a small spring in the middle of the stream bed rather than from the well. Project staff criticised the people for collecting water from the spring rather than water from the well. One woman replied that the spring water was better because it came straight from the ground.

Project staff need to be aware of their own biased views. Collecting water from the spring was easier than lifting it from the well. It would have been difficult to say which was the best quality water without carrying out a water-quality test. We all have our own ideas of what is good-quality water. What we need to decide in each situation is what improvements are necessary to overcome specific, identified problems:

In the case of guinea-worm, the disease is caused by a worm which develops inside the human body. People who are infected are often unable to work and, due to the worm's life cycle, farmers are often affected at the critical time of planting in the fields.

When someone with a guinea-worm in their leg steps into water, or water spills over their leg, the guinea-worm may release larvae into the water. The larvae find their way into small water fleas. Someone collecting water from the same water source may also collect these water fleas. The fleas are then swallowed when the contaminated water is drunk. In the stomach the fleas die but the larvae survive and mature into male and female worms which mate. A year later the

Jan Davis/Oxfam

Sakpuga-kora, Ghana. Swelling on the knee due to guinea-worm infection.

long, developed female worm finds its way through the skin surface. The worm can then lay its larvae into a new water source and the cycle continues. In this way, guinea-worm disease is transmitted from one person to another. If the guinea-worm is prevented from laying its larvae in water, then the disease cannot be transmitted to anyone else.

In areas where guinea-worm disease is common, the main objective of water programmes should be to prevent the larvae being laid, or washed, into water sources. Traditional wells can be protected easily by building a wall above ground level to prevent water containing larvae from being washed into the well.

Any further well improvements to prevent guinea-worm would entail additional inputs which could be better directed elsewhere. For example, putting a handpump on every well would be expensive, take time, and require the establishment of a system of pump maintenance. This extra expenditure and effort might be better spent on constructing more headwalls on open wells and better-drained well aprons. Building less elaborate systems would also make more funds available for hygiene education to make users more aware of the need to improve hygiene conditions around the well.

The best strategy is not necessarily to produce the highest quality water. Rather, it is to *identify the problem* and determine the improvements required to overcome it. The simplest, cheapest method can then be chosen to meet this requirement, and the money saved used to bring wider benefits to more people. The aim should be *'some for all, rather than all for some'*.

1.6 The distribution of benefits

The potential benefits of a programme have been considered as if they were all to be enjoyed equally by the whole community. In reality, however, this may not be the case. Special provision may need to be made for disadvantaged groups of people. Some groups may not be allowed to benefit from an improved supply:

The community of Chefeka, Ethiopia, had a protected spring, but not everyone was allowed to collect water from it. The farmers, weavers, and teachers were, but the tanners, blacksmiths, and potters were not. The latter were discriminated against because of their craft.

The location of an improved supply may have a decisive effect on who benefits:

A borehole was drilled in a village of scattered households near Gambaga, Ghana. Only people living near to the borehole used it regularly. The other households continued to rely on their unprotected traditional wells because the borehole was too far away for convenient use.

If improved supplies are not as conveniently positioned as existing sources they may not be used. In the above example, it was a pity that the money used to drill the borehole was not used instead to line and protect the open wells, which would have benefited more households.

In the case of a sanitation programme, who benefits will depend on who can afford the improvements:

A demonstration project in southern Ethiopia planned to construct a number of latrines in three villages. The idea was that when other households saw the advantages of the new latrines, they would then feel the need to construct similar latrines themselves. However, this did not occur because the latrine was very expensive to build and very few people could afford to have one.

The poorer members of a community may be unable to benefit from a sanitation programme if they cannot afford the building materials.

The benefits to women and children of improving a water supply will vary depending on the circumstances of each project. Supplying better quality water may not benefit everyone if improvements are insufficient to provide easy access to all households. For example, it may be more advantageous for a woman who has little time to spare, to collect water from a poor quality source than to spend time standing in a queue for better quality water.

Children may be given a greater role in collecting water where new water points are closer to homes. This may help hard-working mothers, but increase the workload of children.

Unless specific measures are taken to involve women, it is often men who are introduced to new technology. This can result in men taking over the management of water supplies. Women can then lose control of water sources which they once managed, and become even more dependent on men than they were previously.

Steps can be taken to ensure women will benefit women; benefit to from an improved water supply by establishing well-defined programme aims which will benefit women and encourage their involvement in programme development. Such steps are considered at various points in the book.

Checklist of questions

In the programme with which you are associated:

- What is the programme's general aim?

- What is the community's role in achieving this aim?

- Are hygiene practices considered in relation to the handling and use of water?

- Is hygiene education included in the programme?

- Are existing sanitation practices safe, or is action required to improve the situation?

- Are there particular environmental factors which could affect the development of water sources in the area in which you work?

- Is there an effective way of improving water carrying?

- What is the priority improvement — water quantity or water quality?

- Is access to supplies safe and convenient?

- How are women, men and children each intended to benefit?

- What measures will need to be taken to ensure that different groups and individuals (women, men, the elderly, children, and so on) benefit fairly from improved supplies?

- How will the benefits be measured?

- How will the benefits be sustained?

- Who will pay for the benefits?

Further reading

Boot, M. (1991), *Just Stir Gently: The way to mix hygiene education with water supply and sanitation.* Technical Paper Series 29, The Hague: IRC International Water and Sanitation Centre.

Cairncross, S. and Feachem, R. (1983), *Environmental Health Engineering in the Tropics: An introductory text,* Chichester: John Wiley & Sons.

Cairncross, S. (1988), *Small Scale Sanitation,* 3rd edition, London: Ross Institute of Tropical Hygiene.

Curtis, V. (1986), *Women and the Transport of Water,* London: Intermediate Technology Publications.

Franceys, R., Pickford, J. and Reed, R. (1991), *A Guide to the Development of On Site Sanitation,* Geneva: World health Organisation.

Kamminga, E.M. (1991), *Economic Benefits from Improved Water Supply.* Occasional Paper No.17, The Hague: IRC.

Kerr, C. (ed.) (1990), *Community Health and Sanitation,* London: Intermediate Technology Publications.

Pacey, A. (1980), *Rural Sanitation: Planning and Appraisal,* London: Intermediate Technology Publications.

Winblad, U. and Kilama, W. (1985), *Sanitation Without Water,* Basingstoke: Macmillan.

2

Working together

The relationship between community and agency is central to the development of a community water supply. Many agencies in the past have adopted the position of being 'providers' of safe water. This has meant that the majority of decisions concerning the improvement of a community's water supply have been taken by 'outsiders'. The consequence of this approach is that communities have become dependent on external support to keep improved water supplies working. The responsibility for external support is often passed on to the government water agency on completion of construction.

However, in many countries, long-term government support for the operation and management of water supplies cannot be guaranteed because of a lack of government resources. Communities may then have to take responsibility for managing their own supplies. This means communities must be involved at the outset in taking decisions about how they want to develop and manage their own water supplies.

'Community participation' suggests participation in the agency's water supply programme. But if the community is to have control over the development and management of its own water supply then outside support should be seen as 'agency participation' in the development of a community's water supply. For this approach to be put into practice, however, both partners, community and agency, need to understand each other.

People live together in communities which differ greatly from one another, and have their own customs, traditions, and way of life. Every community is made up of individuals who do not necessarily share the same needs and interests. For example, within any one community there will be some people who are better off than others and therefore their concerns will be different. Women, men and children will all have their own views, especially concerning water, all of which need to be heard. Compromises will have to be made.

Agencies are also many and varied. An agency may be a government authority, a foreign government aid-organisation, or an international or national NGO. Each agency will have its own aims and objectives in developing water supplies. The individuals within agencies will be motivated in different ways and their responsibilities will vary according to their positions. Community members will need to understand these differences and the limitations of each agency.

A community will want to know: who the agency's representatives are, who the representatives' bosses are, what authority the representatives have, why do they want to work with this particular community, how long will they stay for, and many more questions. An agency will want to know the community's system of leadership, consultation, lifestyle, traditions and beliefs.

2.1 Communities and agencies

The success of any programme is dependent on individual people within communities and agencies working together in partnership. This section highlights some of the issues which are important to consider if the community and agency are to work together effectively.

To establish each other's roles and responsibilities, it may be necessary for the partners to produce a formal proposal to develop a supply, and enter into an agreement to manage a supply after construction. It is vital for both partners to understand each other clearly if formal proposals and agreements are to be realistic, appropriate and workable.

Communities

A community may be defined by its ethnic or tribal base, language, religion, or geographical spread:

> *In northern Ghana, an agency carried out initial surveys according to a list of villages named by the chief of a partner community. It became apparent that other villages in the area had not been included. It was discovered that the two groups of villages were from two different tribal and language groups, but living in the same locality. In addition, the initial list of villages covered three administrative areas, which complicated liaison with local government.*

How was the agency to respond? Should the remaining villages in the area be surveyed? Should a programme respect traditional community boundaries or confine itself to government administrative boundaries? There are no straightforward answers but it is clear that careful consultation and agreement is needed with the different groups involved if the later stages of developing supplies are to run smoothly.

Different clan, tribal and ethnic groups may be found within the same community:

Two groups of people lived in the village of Mimpeasam. The larger group had founded the village after migrating to the area. They had their own leader. However, the smaller group was recognised by the local government administration because they had an official claim to the land. They also had their own leader. Both leaders claimed to represent the village. A representative of the larger group approached an NGO for help to improve the village water supply.

How was the NGO to respond? The agency wanted to respond to the community initiative from the larger group but also did not want to ignore the smaller group. An approach to the smaller group might appear to recognise its leader as the village representative, which would upset the leader of the larger group. Officially, the administration recognised the leader of the smaller group and might not be prepared to accept dealings only with the larger group.

In practice, the agency wanted to consult and work with all parties to ensure an improved supply for use by the whole village. A careful, diplomatic approach was needed. A well was eventually dug with participation by people from both groups. It was perhaps fortunate that the site chosen was an equal distance from the houses of both leaders — for technical reasons, of course!

It is worth pointing out at this stage that, whereas the equitable agreement was reached with the leaders of the two tribal groups, there was a range of people in the village concerned with water who may not have been adequately represented by the leaders. In particular, water was a major concern of the women but all the negotiations were with male leaders. Finding ways of consulting with women are considered later.

The importance of water may be so great as to overcome differences within a community; and water can be a focus to bring people together. On the other hand, the issues surrounding water may emphasise divisions within a community. A clear understanding of a community and its customs is needed to avoid conflict and promote cooperation.

Settled and nomadic communities often live side by side and water can become an issue of major concern:

A community in The Affolé, Mauritania, obtained water by digging shallow holes in a dry stream bed. It was an important watering point for both the settled community and nomadic herders with their animals. As part of an NGO aid project, people from the settled community contributed labour and materials to improve the source by constructing a permanent well.

The NGO worked directly with the settled community only, even though the water source was improved at a site where the nomadic community also collected water. Perhaps the following questions should have been asked at the beginning of the project:

- What customary practices and agreements between the settled community and the nomads have there been in the past on the control and use of the existing water sources?

- Have the customary practices always been followed and, if not, what have the problems been?

- Should everyone, both the settled community and the nomads, be allowed to use the well?

- Who should contribute to the construction and maintenance of the well?

- Should water from the well be used for animals, or should it only be for domestic use?

These are just a few of the many questions which should have been answered before the construction work began. It is often easier for an external agency to work with settled communities than with people on the move. There is a danger that nomadic communities can be forgotten, and yet they are often crucial to the development of water sources. Disputes between settled and nomadic communities over water rights are not uncommon. Potential conflicts can be anticipated and avoided through effective consultation.

Before the construction of new supplies, it is important to consider traditional forms of water use and management, in order to build on existing agreements, and not disrupt them.

An example of a settled community sharing an improved supply with nomads can be seen in this case study from Ethiopia:

In the village of Sieru, Borena Region, the Ethiopian Water Works Construction Authority drilled a deep borehole for the people of the village and the nomadic herders, who regularly brought their cattle and camels through the area. The water tariff was set at 10 cents per pot but charges were also levied for the watering of livestock. For example, the water committee charged 20 cents per head for watering camels and 10 cents for cattle. The nomads were allotted times when they could bring their animals to the trough next to the borehole. They paid the committee the agreed amount on a regular basis.

Many remote rural communities may be in the greatest need of assistance, yet are often the last to receive it:

A group of scattered communities living in Sayint, an off-road, mountainous area in Wollo, Ethiopia, made a request to the regional water authority for a hand-dug well. The request was rejected because of the time it would take to transport staff, equipment and materials to the area by mule and donkey. The work would not have been cost-effective compared with work in the authority's main area of activity, along the main roads.

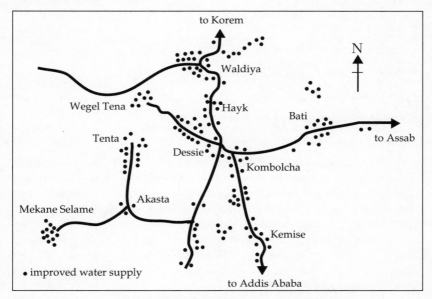

Figure 1 Sketch map of Wollo, Ethiopia, 1985, showing the concentration of improved water supplies along main roads.

Water authorities usually have to achieve annual targets. These may be number of people served, number of wells drilled, percentage of facilities fully working, and so on. It is easier, and costs less, to reach these targets by working with the most accessible communities. This creates a familiar pattern of 'road development', where projects are concentrated along main roads. As a result, remote rural communities are often neglected.

Non-governmental organisations, independent of political pressures, are in a better position than government water authorities to respond to the needs of remote communities. Unfortunately, many NGOs also adopt the above approach, for similar reasons. Poor political and administrative representation makes it difficult for remote communities to make their needs known, and to be aware of what assistance might be available.

Agencies

Just as communities differ, so do agencies. There are several types of agency:

- government agencies
- multilateral agencies
- bilateral agencies
- international non-governmental agencies (NGOs)
- national NGOs
- religious based organisations
- community groups and associations
- private companies such as water companies.

Government agencies include the Ministries, and their departments, responsible for water, health and community development. Government agencies are often short of resources and operate on low budgets. This affects their ability to support and deliver water and sanitation services. Staff may be relatively poorly-paid, and underemployed; motivation may not be high, as a result. However, government staff are often well-trained and have valuable experience, though they often require support and finance to be effective. This may come from external support agencies for specific programmes.

Multilateral agencies include agencies of the United Nations. United Nations Development Programme (UNDP), and United Nations Children

Fund (UNICEF) are active in the water and sanitation sector. They typically support national initiatives and work with government agencies. Activities are often at regional and national level, concerning overall policy and regional planning, rather than direct action at the community level. They can tend to be over-bureaucratic, as they are supported by large funds and personnel from many member countries.

Bilateral agencies are the official development agencies of industrialised countries, that is, government-to-government aid funding such as the Canadian International Development Agency (CIDA). Bilateral agencies usually support government departments, often in specific areas of a country. A recent trend is for some bilateral agencies to contract the running of programmes to private consulting engineering companies who come from the donor country. Staff of these companies tend to operate in advisory capacities as counterparts to government staff. Bilateral programmes tend to be large-scale. This does not always allow for much attention to detail at the community level, as there are a large number of communities to cover in a limited time.

Non-governmental organisations (NGOs) can be international or national. Some international NGOs are not operational themselves, but support other NGOs with funding and training. NGOs usually work below district level and so are able to operate more directly with communities than are the bigger agencies. They tend to be less bureaucratic than bilateral or multilateral agencies.

NGOs rarely work from within government departments, although they do work in co-operation with them and may employ government staff on secondment. By working alongside government departments, NGO programmes benefit from the experience of government staff, who are provided with resources and the incentive to carry out the work for which they have been trained. This way of working also ensures coordination between NGO and government plans.

Community groups and religious organisations operate in a similar way to NGOs. Many international churches receive considerable funds and run large programmes.

Small community groups often rely on external inputs from other agencies in terms of financial, technical and material support. The advantage of small community groups is that they are formed from within the community and they can therefore represent community views closely.

Private water companies may be responsible for larger, usually urban, water supplies. In this situation the community are paying consumers of water and have little further involvement in the supply. However, smaller private companies and individuals may also play an important role by providing expertise and services: building contractors, mechanics, accountants, spare parts suppliers, and so on.

There are differences in how the agencies operate. Government agency staff are often prevented from carrying out effective work in rural areas because of unreliable vehicles and a lack of fuel and funds:

Officers from a Department of Community Development were able to make significant contributions to a rural water programme financed by an external agency. They helped organise, and supported to, self-help water committees. Because of the constraints on government funding, it had been rare for the Community Development Officers to work in situations where both material and technical support were readily available. In the agency-supported programme they had the satisfaction of doing the job for which they were trained.

Many agencies have the resources to support under-funded government services in this way. In this case, the agency could have recruited its own community development staff, as many agencies do. Such an approach might have undermined the standing of the Department of Community Development, and led to staff leaving the department for jobs with the agency, resulting in an even weaker service.

Government staff are often poorly-paid, which results in a lack of motivation. An external support agency may be able to improve this situation, if only temporarily, by improving staff benefits:

On a water and sanitation project in southern Ethiopia, a bilateral agency working with a government water authority increased the daily expense rates of construction crews and extension staff to higher levels. This increased motivation and improved the performance of the government workers.

Problems may occur if only certain members of a government department are attached to an externally-supported programme. Staff who do not benefit will feel even less motivated than before. Such arrangements must therefore be carefully handled.

Agency support may only be short-term, but it can help to increase the experience of staff and the capability of their departments. External agencies can organise training for staff which benefits both the individuals and the departments and communities they serve. These are long-term benefits which are often overlooked.

2.2 Groups and individuals

A community or an agency is made up of many different people. In a community there are:

- leaders: traditional, political, religious;
- professionals: teachers, health workers;
- business people: traders, commercial farmers, water sellers;
- skilled people: craft workers, blacksmiths, carpenters, well diggers;
- a range of people: women, men, children, young, and elderly people;
- the disadvantaged: poor people, lower castes, people with disabilities.

  In an agency there are:

- managers: in the field office, head office, international office;
- professionals: engineers and technicians, community development, health, and financial staff;
- skilled people: supervisors, masons, mechanics, drivers.

These people may all be involved in the development and management of a community water supply. In this section, it is not possible to consider the position of everyone involved but important issues can be highlighted by considering some of the groups and individuals listed above.

Groups and individuals within communities

Within any community there will be a wide range of individuals who will have a particular standing in the community depending on wealth, the position of the family, and the ownership of land, animals or property. In many rural communities there may be 'absent' members: migrant farm workers, educated professionals who work in the towns, traders, and so on, who may be major income earners for the community as a whole. All community members, women, men and children, will have their views about the development of the water supply but some are in a better position to make them known than others. How all their views are heard, and how they will be affected, will depend to a large extent on the approach of the agency.

41

Community leaders

Leaders may or may not truly represent people in a community:

A request to improve the water situation came from community opinion leaders — the chief and local head-teacher. An agency responded and important decisions were arrived at concerning contributions of money, labour and materials. The project seemed assured of full community support from the people.

This is a typical case from northern Ghana. But did the project really have the full support of people from the community? Traditional leaders, chiefs, spiritual leaders, local political leaders and others often have authority which the majority of people are expected to obey. Sometimes this authority means that leaders do not have to explain why their instructions should be carried out. If the reasons are not explained, however, there will be less understanding of, for example, how an improved water supply could improve people's quality of life.

A community leader may volunteer the participation of people in a project without the opportunity for full consultation with the people themselves. Explaining a project to a broader range of people encourages understanding, general agreement, and offers a better chance of real partnership.

There may be conflicts in the community regarding leadership and authority. For example, in the 1980s, the regime in Ethiopia created powerful and unpopular local organisations controlled by central government. This system was often established on top of traditional authority. Such political organisations may enforce activities that the community would not willingly do if they had a choice:

Having assured an NGO field worker of full community participation, the political administrator of Sayint, in Wollo, in the highlands of Ethiopia, enforced intensive community work days for the protection of a spring. The peasant farmers were poor and had little food. They would have preferred to spend their time on their farms. They reluctantly participated through fear of the administrator.

The development of community water supplies in such a situation requires careful negotiation with political appointees and traditional leaders. A realistic approach to the degree of involvement of individuals is needed. Consultation between agency representatives and members of the community could put individuals who express their views in a difficult position with the authorities.

It is therefore important to identify at an early stage the relationship between traditional leaders, political representatives, and the members of a community.

Relations between generations

Different generations often view the same situation in different ways:

> *Extension staff in a village in East Mamprusi District, Ghana, found a disagreement between generations when they were offered a choice in the means of lifting water from a well. The younger people wanted a handpump; the older preferred a rope and bucket. Both groups had strong arguments for each option.*

Why did the different generations have such strong preferences? In this particular area there had been some experience of handpumps fitted on wells several years previously. The older generation had seen them fail, and were content with a simple rope and bucket. However, the younger generation were keen on the best technical option and saw the rope and bucket as a thing of the past. In this case, they were in a stronger position to argue for a handpump as it was they who would do most of the construction work and keep the pump working.

However, in many societies leadership and decision making is a responsibility of the elders. If the younger generation have alternative views it may be difficult for these views to be accepted, or even voiced, due to the respected position of the elders. This applies to both women and men.

The role of caretakers

A caretaker is a member of the community who has the task of looking after a handpump, cleaning a well surround, or being key-keeper of a pump or well. The following is an extract from the evaluation report of a water programme in southern Sudan:

> *'This well was maintained in good condition: channels were clear; vegetation cleared and grass cut short. The caretaker, an old man, was cultivating a vegetable garden. He had even widened the public path leading to the well by himself. He did not allow any litter on the site and water fetchers had to form a queue at busy periods. The users followed his requests, probably because they respected his age.'*

Not all the caretakers were as successful as this man. His approach was very responsible and he probably benefited from his position as caretaker by being able to water his vegetable garden from the well. It appeared he was respected by the collectors because of his age and his dedicated approach to the voluntary caretaker duties.

Sometimes, a woman might be a more appropriate choice for caretaker than a man:

Women were encouraged to be key-keepers in a water programme in Arba Minch, Ethiopia. A key-keeper's job was to open and close a well at certain times of the day. As a regular collector of water herself, and with the same tasks as other women, the key-keeper was always at the well when other collectors wanted to use it.

Wolayta, Ethiopia. Handpump caretakers are important people in water management

Disadvantaged groups

Disadvantaged groups are found in every community. Their status may affect their involvement in decision making and their right of access to water sources:

It was explained in Chapter 1 that the tanners, blacksmiths, and potters of Chefeka, Ethiopia, were not allowed to collect water from the same spring as the farmers, weavers, and teachers. Even the potters, who made the water pots for everyone else, were discriminated against when it came to collecting water!

Disadvantaged groups should be identified and their needs carefully considered during the planning stage, as discussed in the next chapter. In some societies, disadvantaged groups have their own water supply, such as the Harijans in India who have their own wells.

The interests of water-sellers

An improved domestic water supply could have a significant impact on the livelihood of commercial water-sellers. Commercial water-sellers often charge a high price for water. A new, improved water supply would be very attractive to consumers if it was cheaper than buying from a water-seller. However, water-sellers would not be very happy if it meant they went out of business.

Hobyo, Somalia. A water-seller with his donkey cart.

It is not unknown for water schemes to be sabotaged by water-sellers:

In Menna, Bale Region, Ethiopia, water was obtained from a river two kilometres from town. However, most people preferred to buy water from the many water-sellers who transported water in drums on small carts. In 1989 a church agency drilled five boreholes in Menna town. The boreholes were then capped to await the pumps. The installation of the pumps would have meant the end of the water-sellers' business. Later, four of the boreholes were found filled with stones!

45

A lot of money was wasted on drilling the boreholes. It would have been better to have involved the water-sellers from the start, recognising that the wells would put them out of a job. One alternative would have been to offer them jobs as water-sellers at the distribution points that were going to be built around the town as part of the piped network.

Individuals within agencies

Managers

A water programme manager will have many responsibilities, and regular contact with the community may be limited. A government water-agency manager may find it difficult to go far beyond the regional office because of the pressure of administrative responsibilities. An NGO programme manager is likely to be in a very different situation. The NGO programme will probably cover a smaller geographical area and there may be less bureaucracy :

> *An Ethiopian water-authority regional manager became increasingly frustrated with centralised control. During the planning of the annual construction programme the head office would always set an unrealistic target of how many boreholes must be drilled, springs protected, dams constructed, and so on. The targets were always too ambitious. On top of this, the politicians were encouraging community participation without giving the necessary support and training of staff for the new approach.*

Both managers may delegate the tasks of community liaison, but the NGO manager may have the flexibility to establish an approach and engage staff suited to a particular situation. The government manager will be restricted by procedures and established practices.

Extension staff

Extension staff are the people with the important practical task of establishing and developing a partnership between community and agency:

> *An extension agent, recruited from within the Mamprusi community in Ghana, was trained to work with water committees on well hygiene. Her task was to show water committees how to keep their wells clean. On one occasion, a committee member said that, as the agent was paid for her work, she should do the cleaning instead of telling others how to do it!*

There was obviously a misunderstanding. But this does illustrate the importance of clear communication and the difficult role extension staff must play. Extension staff need the public support of both managers and community leaders if they are to be effective. Good communication skills, sensitivity, and diplomacy are essential qualities.

Supervisors

Technical supervisors in rural water supply projects are not just doing a technical job but are also community workers, trainers, and administrators:

Site supervisors in a dug-wells programme in Gambaga, Ghana, provided daily guidance for the construction of hand-dug wells. Typical duties included assisting with the organisation of a daily work rota, training in well digging and lining techniques, and keeping records of the materials used.

Supervisors are key people with a range of skills. They are in a position to encourage the community in their work. However, it is often difficult for a skilled technician to allow someone else, who is unskilled, to do a job which they could do better and faster themselves. Patience, and a commitment to training community members and developing a

Wolayta, Ethiopia. On site discussion between manager, extension agents and technicians is very important for effective teamwork

47

working partnership, are qualities which need to be encouraged. Agencies therefore need to spend time training their technical staff in how to be effective communicators and trainers.

2.3 Tradition, beliefs and attitudes

Agency staff should try to understand the traditions, customs and beliefs relating to water, sanitation, and hygiene behaviour. They should also be aware that their own beliefs may not be shared by the people with whom they work. Hence, an open attitude to both their own, and other people's, beliefs is needed:

> *The village of Zardo in Ethiopia had a newly-protected spring and also a traditional river source. Two women were asked why they chose one source rather than the other. One woman replied, 'the spring water is good, it is clean: the river water is bad, it is brown.' The other woman replied, 'yes, the colour of the river water is brown: but it is flowing, so there is no bad thing in it.'*

Many people grow up with traditional beliefs about good and bad water which, to an outsider, may seem odd. These beliefs will have been passed down from generation to generation. When health educators attempt to change people's behaviour, they need to be sensitive, and have respect for a society's traditional beliefs.

Communities have traditional indicators to distinguish between good and bad water. They may often reject a water with no harmful organisms because of its taste:

> *The Hamar tribe, in southern Ethiopia, dug water holes in the sand bed of a seasonal river. This water was considered clean because it was protected from baboons and hyenas, the perceived carriers of disease. Water from a nearby handpump, however, was disliked because it tasted 'light', and was not good for making local beer.*

People's beliefs can determine whether an improved supply is eventually used, or not. The belief that water should taste a certain way is very important because, for most people, they will have been used to drinking the same water all their lives. When the taste of water is suddenly changed, it seems only natural to be concerned about its quality.

People may not use improved sources if certain customs have not been observed:

In a part of southern Sudan, there was a traditional belief that all water sources had a water spirit associated with them. If the spirit was disturbed, the source would dry up. Failure to perform an appeasement ceremony would upset the spirit. Some people, who strongly held this belief, refused to participate in the deepening of a well in case the water should disappear.

In this programme, the belief was held strongly enough for some people to blame the soil collapse of a well on the anger of the spirit, which had not been appeased. Beliefs such as these should be taken seriously if programmes are to gain popular support. Traditional ceremonies need to be respected. Respect arises from an understanding and appreciation of people's traditional practices:

In the Sudan, a hafir *is a water reservoir dug into black cotton soil. As soon as the soil gets wet it expands and prevents water from passing through it. This provides a good reservoir with very little leakage. The* hafirs *fill with rainwater during the rains to provide a vital dry season storage of water for farmers, and herders with their many camels, goats and sheep. It is, therefore, customary at the end of the dry season for diggers to either dig new* hafirs *or remove silt from old* hafirs *in readiness for the rains.*

Existing forms of water conservation can provide the starting point for further improvements to a water supply. For example, siltation was reducing the storage capacity of *hafirs*. The introduction of controls on farming around *hafirs,* and the inclusion of silt traps at the intake, could have helped to reduce the washing of loose soil into the *hafirs*.

Successful programmes may provide an opportunity for the reconsideration of long-held beliefs:

In the Ugandan village of Kapeka, fish were traditionally connected with water sources. It was believed that as long as there was a fish in the water, the water would not dry up. However, when it came to deepening, lining and protecting a well source, rather than keeping the fish in the well itself, the community agreed that a special pond could be left next to the well for the fish. The well did not dry and so it was accepted that there was no longer a need to keep fish in the well water.

In fact, keeping certain types of fish in open water sources may help to reduce the mosquito population because the fish feed on mosquito larvae in the water. There may be indirect benefits from many traditional practices and therefore advice must be carefully considered before being offered.

Understanding existing practices and beliefs concerning defaecation practices is important to the improvement of sanitation:

The Ministry of Health constructed latrines in some villages in southern Ethiopia. These were individual household latrines. Later, however, it was found that in certain households women were not allowed to defaecate in the same place as men. So, although the men were using the new latrines, the women and children were still using the open-field method.

In this case, it is clear that existing practice should have been more carefully considered before the scheme was implemented.

Checklist of questions

- Who are the groups and individuals in the community with whom you work?

- What measures does the programme take to work with the different groups identified within the community?

- Who are the priority groups?

- Will the benefits of the programme be distributed equally?

- Do existing community leaders represent all community members and, if not, what approach should you take?

- How have women been consulted?

- How have the disadvantaged in society been consulted?

- Are there particular traditions and beliefs that affect programme activities concerning:
  — water?
  — sanitation?
  — hygiene behaviour?

- Has sufficient time been allowed for proper consultation to take place and understanding to be reached between agency and community — in both directions?

- Has a true partnership been established?

Further reading

Eade, D. and Williams, S. (forthcoming) *The Oxfam Handbook for Development Workers*, Oxford: Oxfam. (This is a completely revised edition of the book formerly known as *The Field Director's Handbook.)*

Mosse J.C. (1992), *Half the World, Half a Chance: An introduction to gender and development*, Oxford: Oxfam.

Wallace T. and March C. (editors) (1991), *Changing Perceptions: Writings on gender and development*, Oxford: Oxfam.

PART 2

The programme cycle

The programme cycle

The programme cycle is a series of stages through which the development of a community water supply passes. In Part 2, for convenience, the programme cycle will be followed chapter-by-chapter from planning through to evaluation. In practice, however, the stages of the cycle cannot be divided so easily and are closely interlinked. The way in which the different stages are related to each other is considered in the first chapter of Part 2, '*Planning a Programme*'.

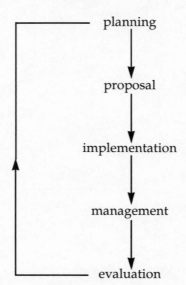

Planning a programme

3.1 The staged approach to planning

Before talking about *Planning a Programme*, some terms need to be explained. The words *programme* and *project* have different meanings. In this book, the word programme refers to an overall framework for the implementation of a series of individual projects. For example:

The original plan for a programme of well construction in northern Ghana allowed for the construction of ten wells in the first year, and 50 wells in each of the second and third years. This gave a total of 110 projects within the three-year programme.

Some agencies are able to respond to individual requests from communities for assistance on a project-by-project basis. Most agencies, however, will tend to work on a programme basis, in which a series of projects is involved. Planning takes place at different levels — at the community project level and at the overall programme level.

Planning stages

There are two key stages to planning. The first stage, *preliminary planning*, involves a period of assessment. The second stage, *detailed planning,* will follow the acceptance of the preliminary plans based on the assessment.

During preliminary planning, the members of the community will want to know what the agency can offer in terms of support in the development of the water supply, and what their own inputs are likely to be. They will also want to know the long-term implications of their commitment, and the future commitment of the agency.

The agency will want to consider how the members of the community feel an improved water supply will benefit them. An identification of how the benefits might be achieved will be essential if the aims of the programme are to be met.

The assessment is carried out in order to identify the problems and plan an overall programme. The programme can be presented in the form of a programme proposal on which the various parties involved need to agree before the programme can go ahead. Detailed planning can follow agreement on the proposal.

The detailed planning stage complements preliminary planning and establishes a framework in which individual projects can be planned at the community level.

Community-initiated or agency-stimulated?

Individual projects may be community-initiated or agency-stimulated. In both cases, if the agency is to respond to community needs the agency must be flexible. The following example, also referred to in the Introduction (p. 4), shows how a community can be involved in the initiation of a project:

In West Mamprusi District, Ghana, an NGO funded an animal traction project to train farmers and their bullocks in ploughing techniques. The training took place towards the end of the dry season in readiness for the rains when land would be prepared. This was a very hot, dry time and water was scarce. It was difficult to obtain enough water for either people or cattle during training. Following lengthy consideration, it was decided the water problem was so great that the community asked the NGO to support a project to improve the water situation.

In this case, the agency was flexible enough to respond to the need for improved water supplies even though the original project was concerned with animal traction.

Community-initiated projects may arise from an ongoing process of consultation between agency and the community. The consultation process aims to work towards the identification of problems inhibiting development in the community. The problems are likely to be wide-ranging. People's desire to improve their water supply and sanitation facilities, therefore, may arise in response to only one of a range of problems which they identify. If the members of the community clearly understand the problems inhibiting their own development, they will be in a better position to initiate projects themselves. They are then more independent and in control than if they had responded directly to an outside agency's view of their problems.

The difference in approach is important in the long term because it will be the community who will have to manage any improvements that are made. A project will be more likely to be successful if, at the beginning, the community is well-motivated through a clear understanding of the likely benefits.

Agency-stimulated projects arise where the agency identifies a geographical area in which to work, having collected information concerning the need for improved water supplies. Programme plans may be based on an estimate of the number and type of projects that the agency is able to fund. An indication of individual communities' needs, and interest in the programme, will become clearer during the preliminary planning stage.

A problem with agency-stimulated programmes can be that the establishment of a target figure of supplies to be built (for preliminary planning and budgeting purposes) establishes a target-led rather than a community-led programme. This must be resisted if a programme is to respond to the problems and needs of a community *at a pace suited to the community*, and not at a pace convenient to the agency.

The first stage of preliminary planning is, therefore, very important. Sufficient funds must be made available for this stage to be carried out well. This may prove a difficulty for some agencies who rely on funding linked to 'numbers of water supplies constructed'. However, there must be a balance between funds for adequate preliminary planning and funds for construction.

Another potential problem connected with the preliminary planning period is the lag between initial consultation with a community and the first signs of active construction work. This may lead to frustration:

Nearly a year had passed between the start of discussions on the improvement of the water supply to the village of Mimpeasam and the arrival of the construction engineer. In the first meeting between engineer and community representatives the engineer wanted to discuss detailed well-design with the users. On realising construction was not going to start that day, one of the elders remarked how disappointed he was that everyone was still talking about the work instead of getting on with it. He left the meeting in disgust saying, 'I will be back when you start digging!'

Frustration at inaction can lead to anger if delays look more like broken promises. Such a response may be due to a lack of understanding between agency and community on the length of time required for preliminary planning. A reasonable balance must be struck between the need for adequate assessment and the community's desire to start the work.

Planning and the programme cycle

Planning, then, is a staged process of preliminary and detailed planning at both programme and community level. Figure 2 is a bar-chart indicating the different programme stages, and shows planning as a periodic activity during this period. The horizontal bars indicate active periods in each programme stage. The example shows an eight-year programme but this period will vary.

Figure 2. An example of a programme cycle: the relationship between planning, proposal, implementation, management and evaluation

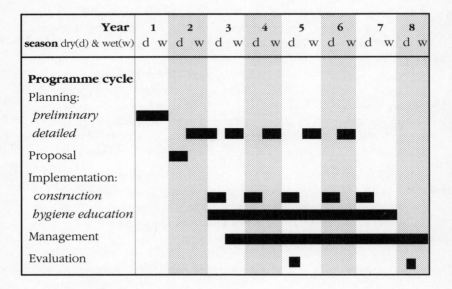

Explanation of the bar chart

The integrated programme of water source improvement and hygiene education in this case spans a total period of eight years. Construction is restricted to the dry season period of the first six months of each year.

- Preliminary planning takes place in the first year, Year 1.

- The proposal is drawn up and agreed in the first half of Year 2.

- The detailed planning of the programme gets under way in the second half of Year 2 and runs into Year 3.

- Construction starts at the beginning of Year 3, at the start of the dry season. Hygiene education is a continuous activity.

- In each subsequent year, detailed planning for individual projects starts towards the end of the dry season and continues through the rains ready for the next dry season construction period.

- Management of the improved supplies by the community begins when the first improved supply has been completed and continues after the agency withdraws support.

- Both a mid-term review and an end-of-programme evaluation have been planned for.

Project selection

It is not possible for an agency to respond to every request for assistance all at the same time. Selection criteria will be required to decide which communities are most in need. The following project selection criteria were established for a spring protection programme in Wollo, Ethiopia:

- The number of people who would benefit from an improved spring — priority was given to those communities with the largest population.

- The return journey time that people had to walk to collect water from traditional sources — priority was given to those who spent the greatest amount of time carrying, and queuing for, water.

- The water quality of traditional sources — priority was given to those communities with the most polluted source.

- The interest of a community in improving their springs — priority was given to those with the greatest interest.

The two extreme cases under these criteria were:

- a large community, with a long return journey time, a source of poor water quality, and a strong interest in improving their spring;

- a small community, with a short return journey time, a source of good quality water, and little interest in improving their spring.

Of course, socio-economic and technical criteria are often conflicting and a balance is not always easy to achieve. For example, some communities may have to walk a long distance to their nearest water source, but this source may be of excellent quality. On the other hand, some communities may have to walk only a short distance to their nearest water source, but this source may be highly polluted.

Additional criteria could be included such as the community's ability and willingness to contribute financially to either the capital cost or long-term management costs of an improved supply. Ability to pay and willingness to pay are very different, and care is needed in separating the two. (See Chapter 6, p. 157, section 6.3 'Financing operation and maintenance' for further discussion of this issue.)

Who decides the project selection criteria?

Communities which are settled, well organised and have good representation will be in a better position to put forward their requests for agency support than less well-placed communities who are perhaps most in need. There must, therefore, be a fair process of selecting projects for support.

Individual communities under one traditional leader or administrative unit may be in a better position to decide priorities than communities which are organised and represented independently. An alternative way of working is for a programme committee to be set up comprising community representatives. A committee may be able to establish a priority listing of communities and to take other decisions affecting communities in a programme. It is evident that a programme committee will only work effectively if committee decisions are recognised and accepted by the respective community leaders.

Agencies may impose their own operational criteria, in addition to socio-economic and technical criteria:

A water programme in Wolayta, Ethiopia, was planned to rehabilitate 25 hand-dug wells each year during a five-year programme. Socio-economic and technical criteria were used to select the 125 proposed projects, but the order in which the projects were to be implemented was related to their geographical location. Construction crews completed work in one district of the region, before moving on to the next district. This avoided working on sites scattered throughout the region at the same time.

Arguments in favour of this approach are that resources can be used more effectively, and staff supervision is easier. However, these apparent advantages need to be weighed against the higher priority of some communities. The community as a whole will be aware of where the more urgent needs are, and the period of preliminary assessment should have identified communities requiring priority support. Priority needs must be taken into account and balanced against the desirability of efficient working methods.

3.2 Gathering information

The process of gathering information provides an opportunity for a community to discuss problems and for an agency to explain how it may be able to help. It is a learning process for both community and agency. The process requires time, staff and money, but is essential if there is to be a sound basis on which to plan an effective and sustainable programme.

The amount of time spent on initial information gathering for the preliminary planning stage must be balanced against:

* the urgency of tackling the most critical needs;

* the cost of information gathering;

* a community's willingness to accept and be involved in the information-gathering process without seeing construction work in progress.

The last point may have an important effect on the long-term progress of a programme. The community may find it difficult to understand why such an exercise is required before construction starts. There may also be a reluctance to respond to approaches for information if the reasons are not adequately understood. A clear explanation of the planning process, and its acceptance by the community, are essential.

Baseline information

Baseline information is information collected before the implementation of a programme. It provides a *baseline* from which a programme moves forward. There are two main reasons for the collection of baseline information:

- to collect information for the preliminary planning of a programme;

- to have baseline information against which evaluation findings can be compared in order to assess whether the programme aims and objectives have been achieved.

The use of baseline information in the evaluation process is considered in the final chapter. Baseline information collected at this stage will be used for future programme evaluation. Likewise, evaluation results from other programmes can be used at the beginning of a new, or extended, programme in both the preliminary and detailed planning stages.

The process of gathering baseline information is as important as the results. It is an opportunity to establish a working partnership with the community. The approach of agency staff must be one in which they are willing to listen, learn and share information with the community.

Sources of information

The information required to plan a programme can be obtained from a combination of sources: government departments, other agencies, and the community itself.

Government departments may have information relating to the programme area, particularly of a technical kind, but it may take time and trouble to locate:

A programme in northern Ghana needed the results of previous test-borehole data. There were no records at the district administration. The regional water department office referred the enquirer to the development project which commissioned the drilling. They replied that all borehole records were kept at the central drilling unit, Kumasi, some 400km away.

Existing information may not be easy to find but effort spent looking for it in the early stages of a programme can save time and be of value in the future. Government departments with potentially useful information will include the Ministry of Health; and Departments of Water, Geology, Mines, Meteorology, Survey, Public Works, and Highways.

It can happen that agencies carry out similar surveys in the same communities. Communities can become impatient with repeated assessment surveys and lack of action, and may then become uncooperative and give poor information. There is often scope for a greater sharing of information between agencies to avoid duplication of effort and expense.

The community itself will be the primary source of information, and the following section indicates some of the methods which can be used to gather the information. A community is made up of many groups of people: women, men, children, the elderly, the poor, the wealthy, the influential, the disadvantaged, and so on. It is, therefore, important that a representative cross-section of the community is involved in the information-gathering exercises if the resulting programme is to fairly represent their needs.

Methods of gathering information

Most agency staff are familiar with answering direct questions; filling in forms; counting, measuring and recording. It seems natural, therefore, to use these techniques when gathering information. However, for many villagers not used to these approaches it is difficult for them to respond in the manner required. People may feel uncomfortable, or even threatened. This example from West Mamprusi District, Ghana, shows what may then happen:

A village questionnaire for household heads was designed to collect basic information on both the human and animal population of each village. After analysis of the results, it became clear that the number of animals recorded was far smaller than the number that could be counted by simple observation.

The survey staff had explained the data would only be used to estimate water demand, so why had inaccurate information been given? There could have been a number of reasons (fears of tax or higher payments for water). An alternative approach was required which encouraged trust and a way for both animal owners and agency staff to find out how much water would be required for animal needs.

People may not feel comfortable giving brief answers to direct questions which then fit neatly on the survey sheet. Real life situations are always more complex than can be given in a 'yes' or 'no' answer. People are more likely to be willing to sit together and discuss an issue. *If the surveyor listens carefully*, the information the surveyor is looking for will probably come out in conversation.

In practice, information gathering is a combination of formal surveys using questionnaires and interviews together with less formal techniques.

The approach should help both partners to learn about the water, sanitation and hygiene situation.

A comprehensive list of methods for the gathering of information would be very long. In this section, some of the methods are briefly mentioned. For further details, see the references at the end of this chapter.

Involving the community in gathering information

Methods of gathering information should try to encourage the participation of people in the community. Informal methods provide a way of sharing the information between agency and community which more formal methods do not easily allow. There are a variety of techniques, referred to by different names including Participatory Rural Appraisal (PRA) and Rapid Rural Appraisal (RRA). (Despite their names, they are not only applicable to rural situations.) The success of the techniques depend on the involvement of a cross-section of people in the community.

One useful participatory technique is called 'community mapping':

In the village of Aruma, Sidamo Region, Ethiopia, members of the community, both women and men, were asked by water authority extension staff to draw a map of their village on a large sheet of blank newsprint paper. The villagers drew an accurate map using coloured pens to show the different features of the village, including all the houses.

This map was then used by the extension staff to discuss with community members various aspects of the village water supply.

It is not even necessary to have a large piece of paper to draw a community map. Maps can also be drawn on the ground, and this can create a great deal of interest, attracting a large number of people to add their comments. In this way, errors can be corrected and different interpretations discussed. Maps drawn on the ground can be transferred on to paper if a permanent record is required.

Community mapping, of the type carried out in Aruma, can be used to identify existing water sources. They can also be useful when the community and agency are discussing the location of water points, such as standposts, and new supplies, such as the site of a well or the route of a pipeline. Further relevant information can also be collected on population, social groups (ethnic, clan, disadvantaged), defaecation areas, access roads, and health facilities.

To find out the changes that take place through the seasons, maps can be altered for each season. Dry and wet season water sources can be identified, areas liable to flooding can be shown. This can help to indicate variations in rainfall, water availability, the time required for water collection, seasonal disease patterns, the busy and slack working periods and so on.

Carrying out the same exercise with different groups of people (women and men, or poor and wealthy people) may show different interpretations of the same situation and give useful insights into a community.

An attraction of these methods is that people enjoy participating in them and it is far more interesting than answering complex questionnaires! The results are there for everyone, community and agency, to see and learn from.

Some wider implications of gathering information

Whatever method, or combination of methods, is chosen, it is important to consider some of the implications of information gathering:

- It requires clear objectives — time, money and effort can be wasted on collecting unnecessary information if objectives are unclear.

- It may raise expectations — activity of any kind, even one visit to a village, may raise expectations, so the reasons for gathering information need to be carefully understood.

- It can take time — enough time should be allowed for preparation, training surveyors, doing the field work and analysing the results.

- It will cost money — sufficient funds must be allocated in programme budgets for gathering information.

- It requires trained and sensitive staff — staff need to be good communicators, listeners, and competent at using techniques which emphasise a partnership approach.

Who gathers the information?

Very often, surveys are carried out by male, urban-based, educated outsiders. Such surveys are likely to result in biases towards their interests, and their concerns, rather than a fair representation of community interests. Involving members of the community as surveyors will help to overcome these problems. Where the divisions between women and men are rigid it is preferable to have women surveyors interview women, and men interview men.

The training of surveyors

Training must be given in how to ask questions, *and how to listen to the answers*. The manner of asking is as important as the content of the questions. Interviewers should be sensitive when asking questions of a personal nature, such as questions about defaecation habits. Training interviewers from within the community will help to overcome some of the difficulties. There should be a system of cross-questioning, that is, asking the same question in different ways more than once, to check the reliability of answers.

When to gather information

Take account of seasonal variations when planning surveys, and analysing data. For example, the quantity of water collected from a traditional source may be used as a criterion for project selection. But this quantity may vary depending on the season:

> *Toward the end of the dry season, about 300 households from the community of Ziban, in the highlands of Wollo, Ethiopia, collected water from a protected spring each day. It was the only spring in the area which did not dry. During the rainy season, however, only about 80 households used the same spring. The remainder collected water from their nearest source: seasonal springs, ponds, or pools of rainwater.*

Seasonal differences in water source data can be extremely marked. Surveys should be planned at appropriate times and may have to be spread over a complete year to be meaningful.

How can women's views be heard?

Traditional forms of consultation need to be respected. They can, however, prevent contact with certain key members of the community:

> *In many traditional West African societies the chief and elders are consulted on every major subject affecting their community. Issues are then discussed, by the men only, at open village meetings until agreement is reached.*

It is usually women who are the main collectors and users of water. Why then are they often left out of decision making when water issues are discussed? It should not be assumed that the subject of women's involvement in village matters cannot be discussed with the men. The way to find out about women and decision making may be to simply ask how, by custom, women do contribute to community matters.

Attempts to hear women's views in situations where women are normally excluded from discussion may not be successful:

In the village of Yirangu, a woman community worker held a meeting with village women to try and discuss their participation in a water supply project. She found it hard to obtain an open response because the women's husbands, who were listening in the background, interrupted and shouted that their wives were saying the wrong thing.

In societies where men have traditionally been in the position of receiving outsiders, they may not approve of direct approaches to women, even if the women meet as a group.

Consultation through traditional women's leaders may be more successful, if allowed, than an approach to a group of women. It recognises the positions of the leaders and establishes an initial point of contact. In some groups, it may be acceptable to talk to older women but not younger women. Older women may have considerable influence but they may not necessarily represent the views of the younger women. Women have busy working days, therefore meetings must be timed so that they are able to attend.

Women's lack of participation in public discussion does not necessarily mean that they do not contribute to community decision making. It may not be appropriate to ask women to give their views in village meetings but their opinions can be sought privately. Even if women are not present at public meetings it does not mean that they do not have a say in decision making in private.

There may be a variety of reasons why men might not want women to be involved in decisions concerning water supplies:

At a village meeting in Bangu, East Mamprusi District, discussions on the siting of a well were nearing completion. The meeting had decided on a site in a valley. Then, almost as an afterthought, the extension worker asked the women for their views. Gradually they spoke up and pointed out that the men had chosen the valley site because they knew that it was going to be easier for them to dig a well at the valley site than at an alternative, but nearer, site. If the well were dug in the valley, women would have to carry water uphill every day; the journey from the other site would be shorter and less steep.

The men were looking at the short-term ease of digging the well. The women were looking at the long-term burden of carrying water. In this case, it was finally agreed to dig the well at the nearer site.

Gerry Garvey

Wollo, Ethiopia. Women extension agents in discussion with a woman collecting water at a traditionally protected spring.

Informal approaches by women extension agents are often the best way of gathering information from women:

Extension staff in Wollo, Ethiopia, spent three days at each of 12 water sources observing the gender and age of water collectors. They found that in their project area, on average, women undertook 90 per cent of all water collection trips, children 8 per cent and men only 2 per cent.

The value of the survey was not so much in confirming that the main collectors of water were women, but that it allowed survey staff to talk directly to women at the water source. Views could be expressed in this natural and relaxed setting. It helped a great deal, of course, that the surveyors were also women. In some societies this would be essential.

The less formal methods of Participatory Rural Appraisal, such as community mapping considered earlier, can be effective in allowing women to make their views known.

In the longer term, consultation on an informal basis is not very satisfactory if women are to be fully involved in the process of design and implementation, although it is better than no consultation at all. If men are not convinced of the need to consult women, then perhaps asking a few straight questions about who collects and uses water most in the community can lead to changes in attitude. Educating men on why it is important to consult with women about a water project might open the way to greater involvement for women in community activities and decision making generally.

3.3 Categories of information

The following section will look at the type of information required for the planning of a community water supply. It is not suggested that all the issues mentioned here should be covered in every programme. Each programme will require different information according to the situation.

The type of information has been divided into two categories: socio-economic information, and technical information. Each category is further divided into separate sections as a convenient way of considering each issue. In practice, information will not be gathered separately but in combination.

Socio-economic information for planning

Level of support

It is important to try to estimate the level of support for development projects:

- Is there a positive feeling in the community about the intervention of an outside agency to help in the improvement of water supply and sanitation facilities?

- To what extent are men and women willing and able to participate in a water programme?

- Have previous attempts been made to improve the water supply and, if so, what happened?

Agencies should, ideally, respond to *community* requests for support, and to the level of community interest in what an agency can offer. However, communities are diverse and a request by one section of the community, or a representative, will not necessarily have the support of everyone in the community.

For example, some people may feel, as taxpayers, that it is the responsibility of government to provide facilities such as water supplies. They may be reluctant to contribute cash or labour. Others may see an aid agency as the provider of the water supply. Their attitudes may be influenced by previous aid programmes in the area.

Priorities will vary. Owners of livestock may be very keen on developing water sources for their animals but an agency may only be looking at domestic water needs. Male farmers, who are often the decision makers, may be more interested in increasing crop yields. Water collectors, usually women, may be hoping to reduce the time and energy spent on getting water.

Ensuring there is genuine support for a project must be a first requirement before further action can be taken.

How many people might benefit from an improved water supply?

An estimate of the number of people who might benefit from a community water supply is an essential starting point for technical design:

> *The objective of the first survey in a water programme in northern Ghana was to estimate the population and the average number of people living in each household. A health survey included an estimate of the average birth and death rates for the area. This gave the population growth rate and, hence, an estimate of the future population size.*

However, as already discussed in Chapter 1, p. 29, section 1.6 'The distribution of benefits', a programme must also consider who in the community will benefit — everyone, including the disadvantaged; the whole or only a part of a village; the poor or the wealthy?

Information on the health of the community

The connections between water, sanitation, hygiene and health were introduced in Chapter 1. If an improvement in the health of a community is a main aim of a programme then it is likely that some specific health problem will have already been identified. Diarrhoea may be considered a big problem, for example. However, it may still be necessary to define the health problems of a community more clearly. To do this, information related to the health of a community will be required:

- What are the diseases related to water, sanitation and hygiene practices?

- How many people have these diseases and who are they?

- Do some people, or certain villages, suffer more than others, and why?

• How severe are other major health problems in comparison to diseases related to water, sanitation and hygiene?

The health status of the community needs to be assessed in order to understand the main health problems:

An NGO water programme worked with the Ministry of Health, Ghana, to carry out a baseline health survey. Two questionnaires were used. One was at village level to collect general information about water sources. The other was at household level to ask families about their causes of illness and death, hygiene practices, and medical care, and the incidence of water-related diseases.

The survey helped to clarify the problems and identify the priority health needs, especially concerning water-related diseases. A programme was then designed to reduce the major problems in the most effective way:

The household survey indicated skin and eye infections were a major problem. The village level survey showed that in most villages there was not enough water during the dry season for regular washing of the body. The overall findings indicated the need for greater quantities of water for washing during this critical period.

In the course of a survey, other health problems may emerge which are not necessarily related to water, sanitation and hygiene behaviour. It is important for the results of surveys to be shared with the Ministry of Health and other relevant departments.

It may be useful to survey villages where no improvements in water and sanitation are planned. These act as 'control villages' against which results can be compared:

In southern Ethiopia, the Ministry of Health carried out a baseline health survey of 16 villages which were to receive assistance to improve water supplies and sanitation. In order to see if there had been a positive impact on health, two villages in the same area that were not going to receive assistance were also surveyed. At the end of the programme the MoH intended to go back and survey all the villages again to find out if there had been any changes in people's health.

As conducting a survey tends to raise people's expectations, the two villages chosen as controls were already included on the list for water supply improvement later in the programme.

Health surveys which aim to measure improvements in community health should be used with caution. There are so many variable factors which affect health besides those associated with improvements to water: hygiene behaviour, sanitation, health services, food availability, and the state of the local and national economy.

A problem with many health surveys is that they expect too much from the respondents. If, for example, diarrhoea commonly occurs in the household it will be difficult for respondents to remember and count the occurrence of all cases of diarrhoea beyond a few weeks back. What is meant by 'diarrhoea'? Is a distinction made between diarrhoea and dysentery for the purposes of the survey, and how do the community distinguish between them? A survey must be clear about the information it is asking for.

In the past, evaluations have tried to assess the impact of a programme by measuring changes in the severity of diseases before, during, and after water supply and sanitation improvements. However, these studies have often failed to give clear results. It is now felt that a better measure of a programme's impact is to look at changes in behaviour, such as the washing of hands before handling food, and the safe disposal of excreta.

Information on people's awareness of the connection between water and health

In order to assess the need for hygiene education, it is important to find out people's existing beliefs about water and health:

- What do women, men, and children know about water-related diseases?

- What are the attitudes of women, men, and children towards handling and using water?

Information on how people believe they become ill and the measures they take to protect themselves should be a part of the preliminary assessment. Health and hygiene education can then be planned based on this information:

During a meal break in the work on a well in northern Ghana, the well supervisors were offered water to drink from the village 'dug-out'. This source was open to pollution from rainfall run-off, and animals, so they refused to drink it and explained why. The host was very upset and argued that since the food they were eating contained plenty of pepper it would protect them from any upset stomach. They should not be afraid to drink the 'dug-out' water.

Wolayta, Ethiopia. How aware are women, men, and children of the connection between water and health?

A health education programme should first establish people's understanding of water, health and hygiene.

Information on existing sanitation practices

Before any measures can be taken to improve sanitation it will be necessary to gather information on existing practices. How information about this is obtained will depend on how acceptable it is to discuss the subjects of sanitation and human excreta within a community. Community mapping methods may be used to indicate defaecation areas within a village — the zones for women and for men. Further discussion may lead on to sanitation practices, customs, and beliefs. The socio-economic information needed to plan sanitation improvements will include:

- attitudes towards excreta;

- customs related to defaecation;

- the needs of women, men, children and the elderly;

- how high a priority is given to improved sanitation by the community;

- how attitudes vary between community members.

Enlisting the support and interest of community leaders can be a way of finding out about what is acceptable in a community. The support of community leaders may also help to establish the idea of improved sanitation and encourage further interest within the community:

In a pilot sanitation programme supported by the Ministry of Health, Ghana, and a bilateral aid agency, community leaders were involved at the early stages of finding out the best and most acceptable form of improved sanitation. In one village, the religious Imam was very enthusiastic and constructed three different types of latrine in order to test which was the best design.

Information on water collection patterns

In each community there will be a fairly regular pattern of water collection. It is useful to know when water is collected throughout the day for both technical and social reasons. For example, a well or spring will need to have a yield sufficient to supply water at the peak collection times. It might be necessary to shut down a piped supply to standposts during slack periods to allow for the storage of water for supply at peak collection times. Knowing these periods will assist technical design and the appropriate management of supplies to match users' needs.

Water containers tend to be standardised within a locality. Average volumes can be used to estimate the amounts of water collected at a source by simply counting the number of containers filled:

A team of survey workers monitored the collection of water from a traditional source at Boneya, Wollo, Ethiopia, from early morning to early evening. They estimated the total quantity of water collected by counting the number of collectors coming to the source each hour, and assuming each adult collected 20 litres and each child 10 litres. Presenting the results on a graph clearly showed the pattern of water collection during the day, and the number of people collecting water each hour.

Figure 3: Water collection pattern at Boneya, Wollo, May 1989

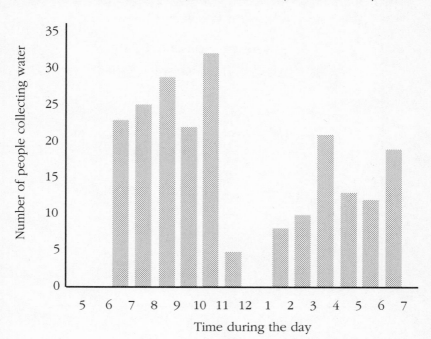

Figure 3 shows the two main collection periods between 6am and 11am in the morning and 3pm and 7pm in the afternoon. The peak collection hour was between 10am and 11am.

Information on the quantity of water collected

How much water is collected for each woman, man, girl and boy in a household? A programme might aim to increase the quantity of water used by each person in the community. Information collected on a periodic basis can give an indication of the trends in water consumption and can be compared to baseline survey estimates of how much water per household was collected from traditional sources before the programme began.

Surveys at a water source can give an estimate of household water use:

> *At Boneya, survey workers recorded the name of each collector's head of household as they came to fetch water. The number of people in each household, their age and gender were also recorded. The*

quantity of water collected for each household was recorded over a period of one week. The total was averaged to give the amount of water collected per day for each person in the household.

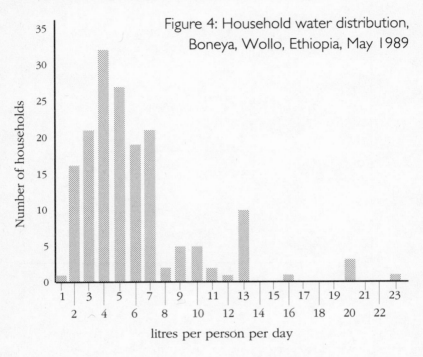

Figure 4: Household water distribution, Boneya, Wollo, Ethiopia, May 1989

litres per person per day

Figure 4 shows that the water collected by the 167 households ranged from 1-23 litres per person per day with a mean of only 5 litres per person per day. The amount collected by each household could also be found from the original data.

Information on the time spent collecting water
The time it takes to collect water is an important consideration in assessing priority needs:

- How far do women and children have to walk to collect water?

- How much time do they spend walking to and from the water source?

- How much time do they spend queuing at the water source?

When asking about times and distances to water sources, surveyors should be aware that villagers may have a different concept and means of measuring time and distance than do outsiders who design questionnaires. Surveyors must visit water sources themselves to get accurate information.

Estimating return journey times to and from a water source can help in identifying those communities who have the hardest task to collect water:

> *At Boneya, an estimate of return journey time for each household was obtained by survey workers walking with water collectors from sources to a number of houses in the community and recording the time taken. These houses were then used as a reference in estimating the time taken by other households. These times were only walking times to and from the source, and did not include waiting time at the source, which were recorded separately.*

Figure 5: Return journey time to collect water at Boneya, Wollo, Ethiopia, May 1989

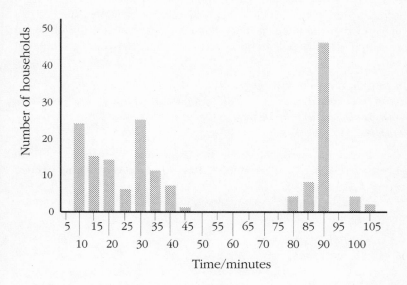

Figure 5 shows that, of the total number of 167 households, 103 had a return journey time of 10-45 minutes, and 64 households had a return journey time of 80-105 minutes. In this example, it was clear that a priority was to locate a new source — a dug well — near to the 64 households.

Information on money matters

It is rare for individual rural communities to be able to afford the total cost of improving a water supply. The critical issue is usually whether the community can afford the cost of operation and maintenance in the long term. Therefore, information is required to determine:

- How much is the community willing and able to contribute to construction, operation and maintenance costs?

- How is money collected and saved for community purposes?

- What are the customary savings schemes of both women and men, and how will these affect financial management?

- Who controls income and expenditure in the household — women or men — and how might this affect the management of water supplies?

Surveys on the local economy and the average wealth of a household are complex to carry out and can take a lot of time. Specific localised surveys could supplement government figures but may be more appropriate during the detailed planning phase. Traditional methods of saving and rural banking facilities should be considered during initial surveys, and also the skills required for local financial control should be identified:

In Ghana, a scheme was proposed whereby villages were given bank loans, guaranteed by an aid agency, to hire a contractor to construct wells. The loans were to be paid back through regular payments over a period of years.

This required a capability within the community to manage the loan finances. Surveys had to determine existing skills and the training needed to run such a scheme within each village.

Money will be required for materials in order to sustain the simplest improved supply:

On completion of each well, in a programme in northern Ghana, the support agency sold communal buckets and nylon rope to the well users. From time-to-time buckets and rope had to be replaced as they wore out and communal funds had to be found to pay for them.

In some societies, traditional savings schemes may be used to finance the regular replacement of items to keep a supply working, such as the buckets and rope in the case above.

As women are the main users of water supplies, they are usually keen for them to be maintained. However, because of conflicting demands, women may have problems in obtaining money where men have control of household funds. Women's concern for the upkeep of a water supply may not be rated highly by the men in comparison to other needs.

Information on community structures

Some assessment needs to be made of community ability to manage an improved water supply:

- Is the community willing and able to manage an improved water supply?

- Do appropriate management structures exist?

- Are people with management skills available?

- Are any of these people women?

- What additional training will be required?

Initial surveys might consider: existing structures, the representation of women and disadvantaged groups, and past successes and failures in community management. These points are briefly mentioned here because they need to be considered at the preliminary and detailed planning stages so that an appropriate strategy can be developed to ensure successful community management of completed supplies. These issues are considered further in Chapter 6, 'Managing community water supplies'.

Technical information for planning

The kinds of technical information needed for planning will include the physical characteristics of the area and the type of existing water sources. Information will also be required concerning the availability of skills, materials, and equipment. It is important to gather information about the following:

- the hydrology, geology and topography of the area;

- existing water sources;

- water quality;

- the effect of the seasons;

- the availability of local technical skills;

- the availability of construction materials;
- local services.

The hydrology, geology and topography of the area

- Hydrology: where can water be found, when, and how much?
- Geology: what is the soil and rock type and how does it vary?
- Topography: what is the shape and form of the land — hills, valleys, and plains?

First of all, find out what relevant information already exists:

No rainfall records were obtained when a roof rainwater-harvesting system was designed and installed in Hararghe, Ethiopia. Instead of providing enough water for the whole community, the constructed systems only served a few households during the dry season. Most people lost interest in the project when they realised they would not benefit. The constructed systems quickly fell into disrepair and were abandoned.

The roof rainwater-harvesting systems were adopted by the programme simply because staff believed there was a lot of rain in the area. Nobody took the time to check the rainfall records in the first place. The government department responsible for water supply is usually a good place to start.

Information can sometimes be found in unlikely places:

In Sudan, rainfall records had been kept for decades by railway station supervisors as part of their regular duties. As a consequence, records covered a large part of the country wherever the railway went. Unfortunately, they stopped abruptly one year when the supplement for the task paid to the supervisors was taken away as part of a government cost-cutting exercise!

General records, where they exist, will give some indication of the depth of the water table and the yield of springs. However, the depth and yield will vary throughout the year according to the season, so it is most important to relate information to the time of the year it was collected. A well full of water in the wet season may dry during the dry season.

A lot of useful information can be obtained from simply asking people who live in the area. Local farmers will have very detailed knowledge of rainfall patterns, river and stream flows, soil conditions, and the

Jenny Matthews/Oxfam

Wollo, Ethiopia. Hand augers are simple to use.

availability of construction materials. It is important to involve the community in technical surveys where possible. Village teams can be trained to use a hand auger to gather useful information on the presence of groundwater and soil types:

As part of well-digging projects in both Ghana and Ethiopia, tests were carried out to determine groundwater levels and the types of soils, using a hand auger. The auger was a simple drill with a range of auger bits operated by hand by just two people. A different bit was used to auger through different types of soil. Extension rods allowed depths of up to 15 metres to be reached.

After a short period of training, the community can be left to carry out their own investigations. The use of a hand auger is limited in rocky sites, but although it cannot penetrate hard rock it is still able to show where, and at what depth, rock will be met.

There may be local methods of finding water:

The supervisor of a church-funded water programme in northern Ghana used his water-divining skills to locate well sites. The method involved walking over the ground with a swinging pendulum. When the pendulum reacted in a certain manner it indicated water was to be found below ground.

The programme appeared to have a reasonable success rate. The success of water diviners will vary and much may depend on local conditions.

Information on existing water sources

It is important to obtain answers to the following questions:

- Where do people currently get their water from?

- What condition are these sources in?

- How do the sources vary throughout the year?

In order to improve the supply of water it is necessary to find out where people obtain their present water from. This might at first appear straightforward. Simply ask people. But who? Tradition can restrict consultation to male leaders only. They may not be fully aware of all the water sources used by women. It is the women who know where they fetch the household water from. Therefore, any enquiries need to involve the women who usually fetch water.

Only the sources currently being used at the time of the survey might be mentioned. The situation at each critical time of the year, such as the end of the rainy and dry seasons, should be checked. Water for drinking and cooking, and water for body and clothes washing, are often collected from different sources; and this needs to be clarified.

People skilled in traditional well digging and the protection of water sources will obviously be important people to consult.

Information on water quality

The quality of water obtained from existing supplies needs to be assessed:

- How is the quality of water measured?

- Can water quality be tested in the field?

Water quality is only one factor in the reduction of water-related diseases. However, it is an important factor. Water quality surveys can help to identify those sources which are most heavily contaminated and require high priority attention.

The quality of a water is determined by physical, micro-biological, and chemical factors. *Physical* factors include taste, smell, colour and turbidity (how cloudy the water looks). The physical aspect of water is what users often consider the most important, because it is what they use to compare one sort of water with another. *Microbiological* contamination of water is by invisible organisms, such as bacteria. *Chemicals* occur naturally in water, but some can be harmful in high concentrations.

A combination of observation, local knowledge and scientific water tests will give information on the quality of different water supplies.

Microbiological water-quality testing: A brief background to microbiological water-quality testing is given in Appendix 1, p. 169. Further information can be obtained from the references given at the end of this chapter.

Unfortunately, there is no simple, easy method of testing the microbiological quality of water in the field:

> *At a conference on rural water held in Accra, Ghana, the subject of water quality testing arose. Laboratories were unable to monitor village supplies because they lacked transport and field equipment. It was suggested that communities themselves should be involved in checking their own water supply. The suggestion was that teachers and traders could carry water samples to the laboratories when travelling to town. The idea sounded good but could not work because of the technical and practical problems involved.*
>
> *Some of the problems were as follows. The number of bacteria in water will change over time; if water is tested many hours after collection, the sample will not truly represent the quality of the source. If the sample container is not sterilised it will pollute the water, and it will be the quality of the container as well as the water that will produce the results. It would not be easy for a village firstly to find a sterile container and then to get it to a laboratory in time for a test. The laboratory should test the sample as soon as it arrived; for many district and regional laboratories this would be difficult to do.*

However, even in remote areas with no access to a public health laboratory, it is possible to test the bacteriological quality of drinking water if the equipment is available:

> *A spring protection programme in Ethiopia wanted to record baseline water quality data from traditional water sources in off-road, mountainous areas. The sources were several days journey from the nearest public health laboratory. Bacteriological water quality was tested using a portable water testing kit weighing about 10kg and carried in a frame on someone's back. The battery was recharged every week from a solar panel.*

Portable water quality test kits provide a very convenient and effective method of measuring the bacteriological quality of field water sources. However, as this kind of equipment is expensive it is only worthwhile for an agency to purchase a test kit if regular use will be made of it, and a supply of chemicals can be ensured. Staff can be trained in the use of

Wollo, Ethiopia. Bacteriological water quality can be tested in remote rural areas using a portable test kit

such kits in only a few days.

Chemical water quality: The presence of chemicals in water can cause water to taste unpleasant, or can cause more serious health problems. Information on the general chemical quality of water should be sought from a government water agency.

In some areas, iron can be found in high enough concentrations to give groundwater an unpleasant taste. It can give a brown colour to food, and stain clothes. Although not harmful in itself, the danger is that safe water with a high iron content is often rejected in favour of highly-polluted surface water.

Salty water may be found in certain areas. It is not practical to remove salt from rural water sources and other sources will have to be investigated.

Fluoride can be harmful in high concentrations. It can stain children's teeth brown and can affect bone growth. Fluoride cannot easily be removed from water. In high-fluoride areas it is important to note the variety of possible sources, and their different fluoride concentrations, so that appropriate choices of supply can be made. However, the right choices may not be made:

> *In the town of Awassa, southern Ethiopia, there are many shallow wells which produce water with a high fluoride content. The town's piped water supply has a lower fluoride content but the well water is preferred because it is free.*

Information about the quality of different water supplies can provide the basis for a decision to organise a health education campaign.

Unprotected — and even galvanised steel — handpump riser pipes can be eaten away by 'aggressive water', which is usually acidic. However, it is not just the effort and expense of replacing lost steel parts which is a problem:

> *In southern Ghana, the corrosion of steel pump rods and rising main pipe can lead to an overnight build up of iron in well water. The iron concentration can be so great that users reject the water because of its bitter taste. The result is that people go back to using their old polluted sources.*

To avoid corrosion problems, stainless steel, plastic and other non-corrosive materials can be used in parts likely to come into contact with aggressive water:

> *In Luwero, Uganda, aggressive spring water resulted in the complete corrosion of spring outlet pipes in only two to three years. To solve this problem, plastic PVC pipe was placed inside the galvanised steel outlet pipes. The PVC protected the steel from corrosion and the steel pipe protected the plastic pipe from physical damage.*

It is important to note the presence of aggressive water at an early stage of a programme so that its presence can be taken into account in programme planning.

Information on seasonal variations

Heavy rainfall can result in flooding, muddy conditions, high groundwater levels, high spring yields, and large stream and river flows.

Seasonal variations in the water table must be considered by both sanitation and water programmes:

> *The first pit latrine constructed in the village of Kubore, Ghana, was nearly completely flooded in the wet season owing to the rise in the groundwater level. Waterlogged soil also seeped into the pit, leading to subsidence. The water table fell only slowly after the rains and this encouraged mosquito breeding in the pit far into the dry season. Following this experience, those managing the programme had to reconsider their ideas on sanitation.*

There can be general drainage problems in areas with a high water table, because soakaways may flood. In addition, soakaways may simply be unable to cope with normal drainage water increased by large quantities of heavy rainfall run-off. These conditions will affect technical designs.

The effect of seasonal changes, especially the onset of the rains, may mean that construction activities will have to stop for a period of months. It is therefore important to collect accurate and reliable information on rainfall, and the timing of critical changes in the seasons, as part of the planning process.

The type and extent of local technical skills

Agencies must not overlook the skills available within communities:

> *Local well diggers can be found in many villages in southern Ethiopia. In one village, well diggers charged 9 birr (US$4) per metre to dig a well in clay. They used buckets for dewatering, and the wells were left unlined.*

For the construction of improved, lined wells, traditional well diggers may require training in upgrading and adapting their skills to longer-lasting and more sanitary designs using permanent materials, such as concrete. Training will need to be allowed for in planning.

On larger programmes there may be issues concerning labour laws, minimum wages, and safety issues to consider:

> *A bilateral donor agency wanted to employ local well diggers in a programme in Ethiopia. However, the government water agency maintained that the union would not allow local, non-government, workers to dig wells for which the water agency were supplying the materials.*

These issues need to be taken into account at the planning stage. The employment of local artisans such as well diggers, masons, blacksmiths, and so on, has the added advantage of contributing to the local economy:

> *A sanitation programme in northern Ghana, supported by a bilateral agency, included the training of local masons in the construction of concrete latrine squatting-slabs. The masons working in the area could then employ these new skills and ideas locally for the benefit of themselves and the community.*

It is important to identify, at the early planning stage, not only the availability of local skilled artisans, but also the basis on which they are willing to participate in community programmes. The employment of skilled artisans in community projects could pose problems where voluntary contributions of labour are expected. This must be worked out within each community.

The type and extent of locally available construction materials
The location of construction materials can affect programme implementation:

> *At the beginning of a new well-digging project in northern Ghana, a manager found no locally available rock suitable for concrete or the stone lining of wells. During the preliminary assessment phase, not enough consideration had been given to where the construction materials might come from. As a result, there were not enough funds allocated to pay for the purchase and transport of sand and stone.*

Communities may need assistance to collect and transport materials if these are not locally available. Negotiations may be necessary with landowners or traditional guardians of the land where sand and stone are located. Failure to follow local customs regarding land rights and access to materials could severely disrupt a programme.

All these issues of material location, ownership, access rights and local customs need to be considered during the initial programme assessment.

Local services
Those planning a programme will need to take account of the services required which are locally available:

• suppliers of tools, equipment and spare parts;

• local building contractors;

• transport;

- workshops for making and/or repairing equipment.

The support of local services by both smaller and larger agencies can be of advantage to everyone:

Two agencies supported hand-dug well programmes in adjacent districts of northern Ghana. Both agencies required additional well-lining shuttering after having already imported moulds at great cost. They approached a small factory making agricultural tools, who were able to make prototype shuttering. After initial trials, modifications were made and the design soon became popular with other well-digging programmes in the region.

Co-operation between the two programmes made it cost-effective to finance the prototypes. The factory found new customers for the shuttering from other agencies. The programmes, factory, and the country all benefited.

International agencies, in particular, have a tendency to import equipment without fully considering local alternatives. Identifying local suppliers can avoid unnecessary importation of equipment and help to support local skills and enterprise within a region. This reduces dependence on external assistance.

Plans need to be made for the transportation of equipment and materials in remote rural areas:

Equipment and materials for construction had to be transported in mountainous areas of Ethiopia. Clearing tracks for vehicles was out of the question because of the rough terrain. Pack animals such as donkeys, mules and camels had to be used, and hire arrangements made with the local owners of animals.

3.4 Technology and design

Once the technical, social and economic information has been gathered during the preliminary assessment it will be possible to identify appropriate water supply and sanitation choices. Later, at the detailed planning stage, the design of each water system can be finalised in consultation with each community, to take account of users' preferences.

This section looks at the technology choices which will have to be made, and the importance of involving the community in technical design.

Technology options

It is not intended to go into detail concerning small-scale community water supply and sanitation technologies. There is already a good range of information available, and references are given at the end of this chapter. However, it is useful to summarise the water and sanitation options and to consider certain technology issues.

Groundwater sources	Surface water sources
protected springs	reservoirs
dug wells	ponds
hand-drilled wells	streams and rivers
machine-drilled wells	

Generally, groundwater is of a higher quality than surface water and therefore requires less treatment, if any, before it can be supplied as drinking water.

All the above sources ultimately rely on rainwater. The direct collection of rainwater from roofs and gutters can be an important source, in itself, for individual households and institutions.

Treatment

Water treatment methods for small-scale community supplies must be simple to operate and maintain, and involve the minimum use of chemicals, if any. Treatment methods are usually restricted to simple storage and settlement.

Pumped supplies

In the case of groundwater sources, water may need to be pumped from below ground. In the case of all sources, water may need to be pumped to the point of use. Power for operating pumps can be provided by:

- hand — handpumps

- foot — pedal and foot operated pumps

- windpower

- solar power

- diesel or petrol engine
- electric motor

Piped supplies

Water may need to be piped from the source to the point of use. In a basic system, a piped supply will include a storage tank, pipeline for distribution, and one or more standposts. A community can undertake the general day-to-day operation and maintenance of a simple piped supply but may require back-up from a water authority for major repairs.

Sanitation

Sanitation technologies range from the simple dry-pit latrine to the water-flushed toilet. In many rural and poorer communities, water is not available for flushing. Limited amounts of water are used in the pour-flush latrine but the system is still more expensive than a simple dry latrine. The ventilated improved pit (VIP) latrine is commonly recommended as a low-cost sanitation solution where conditions are favourable.

Appropriate technology

The term 'appropriate technology' is often misused because technology which is often called 'appropriate' may not always be applied in an appropriate way. There are many examples of technology which has been applied without full consideration of how it can be kept working when it breaks down:

> *Degagabub refugee camp on the Ethiopia-Somalia border relied on a series of shallow wells in a sand river bed for its drinking water supply. The sun shone most of the day, nearly every day of the year. This combination of circumstances seemed ideal for a solar pumping system. One day, the pump broke down. As the camp was in a remote area, with no maintenance facilities, the pump was taken to the nearest town. The mechanics in the town were very familiar with diesel engines, but the sealed unit of the solar pump was something new. The manufacturer of the pump had no service agent in the country but offered to replace the unit. However, it would take several months to deliver.*

Was a solar pump 'appropriate' in this case? Before introducing new technology, it is wise to investigate the available support services and to consult with the government water agency about long-term operation and maintenance.

Standardisation

Agencies should support the standardisation of equipment:

A government water agency in southern Ethiopia undertook a survey of all handpumps in its region. It found nine different types of handpump from nine different countries.

The use of many different models of the same equipment creates operational and maintenance problems. Standardisation has the following advantages:

- People become familiar with standard equipment and get to know how to install, use, maintain and repair it well.

- The training of staff and users is simplified because the training need only be concerned with standard equipment.

- The supply of spare parts for standard equipment is easier than having to supply parts for many different models.

Proposals for a new programme should try to specify the type of equipment which is already in use in the region, to support standardisation.

Gerry Garvey/Oxfam

Water Supply and Sewerage Authority Southern Regional Office, Awassa, Ethiopia. The need for agencies to support the standardisation of equipment is clear.

Technology choice:

Following the preliminary assessment, technology choices will need to be narrowed down to produce a budget estimate and plan for a programme proposal.

To take a springs and wells programme as an example; the technical and material support for the protection of springs will be different from that for the construction of dug wells. The preliminary assessment will indicate which options are possible and the likely mix of springs and wells. Funds will need to be allocated for these and general plans drawn up. The detailed design of each spring or well can then be decided at the detailed planning stage by each community with advice from the agency.

The technical choices that an agency will be able to support will depend on two factors: the technical resources available to them; and their technical competence in using them. There may be a range of options open to the community.

It is important that the advantages and disadvantages of each technology are understood. Communities want to know exactly what the risks and costs will be of different options:

A project in northern Ghana supported by a bilateral agency offered a choice of water supply; a hand-dug well or a drilled borehole. The costs and benefits of each system had to be carefully explained in advance, as it was a complex choice for a village to make.

Hand Dug Well	Drilled Borehole
High participation by the community in construction	Low participation by the community in construction
Low to medium construction cost: medium cost community contribution	High construction cost: high cost community contribution
Handpump not needed to lift water	Handpump needed to lift water
Completed as a closed well, fitted with a handpump: water quality high	Fitted with a handpump: water quality high
Completed as an open well: liable to pollution	If handpump breaks there is no other alternative
Maintenance cost low	Maintenance cost high

The most appropriate choice should be *the system that a community can both afford and manage so that when there is a problem the community can solve it with the minimum of outside assistance.*

Community participation in construction may sound a good thing but will it help long-term community management? The answer is yes, if it helps a community to understand how a system operates and how it can be maintained in the future.

Detailed design

Detailed design will tend to concentrate on the above-ground components with which users will come into regular contact and for which they will be directly responsible. Designers need to consult with the main users of water supplies — women:

> *During a meeting in Sayint, Wollo, Ethiopia, between a woman extension agent and a group of women, one of the main issues discussed was the difficulty of placing a pot full of water onto someone's back. It was especially difficult when a woman was alone at the well, with nobody to help her with the initial lift. Various suggestions were made to improve the standard design of well. Finally, it was agreed that a masonry wall would be built around the well. Women could place their pots on the wall as a help in loading them onto their backs.*

In addition to helping women and children in placing their clay water pot onto their back, a durable masonry wall also prevented cattle from walking over the cover slab, damaging the handpump, and defaecating in the immediate surroundings of the well.

Gerry Garvey/Oxfam

Wolayta, Ethiopia. A small wall next to the water point helped women and children to lift heavy water pots onto their backs.

Involving users in design can result in facilities being more practical and popular:

Technical staff of a water programme in Ghana built a raised platform for washing clothes in the village of Kubore. The platform had been designed so that washers could stand up to wash. The platform was also sloped to assist the drainage of waste water.

After some use, specific concerns were raised by the women about the washing platform. They said that when they washed clothes on the sloping platform all their soapy washing water easily drained away. This meant they used too much expensive soap. The design also meant they could not use their washing bowls as they did not sit well on the platform. They preferred an alternative design which was simply a flat slab of concrete on the ground. This provided an area which could be easily cleaned and allowed the women to place their bowls on a flat surface.

In this case, it was possible to introduce some simple modifications of the design which took account of user preference.

Checklist of questions

- How did your programme begin?

- Has sufficient information been gathered on which to base an initial programme proposal?

- What kind of information is required?

- Does your agency have the capacity to carry out surveys or will it have to look for assistance from outside?

- Who is going to design, implement and analyse the survey information?

- Your programme may have already started with insufficient information. What can you do about it?

- How are members of the community involved in the information-gathering process?

Further reading

Boot, M. T. and Cairncross, C. (eds), (1993), *Actions Speak: The study of hygiene behaviour in water and sanitation projects*, The Hague: IRC

Wolayta, Ethiopia. Design for the convenient use of water collectors.

International Water and Sanitation Centre and London School of Hygiene and Tropical Medicine.

Franceys, R., Pickford, J., Reed, R (1991), *A Guide to the Development of On-site Sanitation*, Geneva: WHO.

Hofkes, E.H.(ed.) (1983), *Small Community Water Supplies: Technology of small water supply systems in developing countries.* Technical Paper Series No.18, The Hague: IRC. Also available in French.

Lloyd, B. and Helmer, R. (1991), *Surveillance of Drinking Water Quality in Rural Areas*, Longman, England.

McCracken, J.A., Pretty, J.N., and Conway, G.R., (1988), An Introduction to Rapid Rural Appraisal for Agricultural Development, London: IIED (International Institute for Environment and Development).

Nichols, P. (1991), *Social Survey Methods*, Development Guidelines, Oxford: Oxfam.

Oxfam Well Digging Manuals Pack (1992) — includes the manuals on the Survey Auger Kit, and the Delagua Water Testing Kit. Oxford: Oxfam.

Pacey, A. (1980), *Rural Sanitation: Planning and appraisal*, London: IT Publications.WHO (1985), *Guidelines for Drinking Water Quality; Vol.3: Drinking water quality control in small community supplies*, Geneva: WHO.

4

Preparing a proposal

A proposal is the written summary of a planned programme. It is a reference document to which all parties involved in a programme can refer. Such a document is often required by agency head offices, donors, and governments before a programme can be accepted for funding, or is allowed to proceed.

This chapter looks at how a written proposal can be drawn up based on the appraisal of the information gathered during the preliminary planning stage.

4.1 Reviewing the information

The information gathered will have identified problems related to the existing water and hygiene situation. Other major problems may also have been identified, for example in respect of agriculture, and these should be referred to the appropriate agencies.

The first decision is whether to do anything at all. The capability of different agencies varies a great deal. For example, mechanical drilling for water may have been identified as the only way of improving the existing water supply. However, drilling can be a major undertaking which could be beyond the technical and funding capacity of a small agency.

An agency has to be realistic about the extent to which it can assist. The level and type of assistance will always depend on the combined resources of the agency and community. An agency may not have the technical capability to improve water sources, but it may still be possible to support hygiene education and sanitation improvements. In some cases, hygiene education could be the major component of a 'water supply programme'.

An alternative to full commitment to a programme is to propose a short pilot programme:

A bilateral development agency in East Mamprusi District, Ghana, wanted to complement their drilling activities with a hand-dug well component to the programme. However, there was little experience of dug wells in the area and so a small-scale pilot project was carried out in the first year. The advantage of this approach was that it provided direct field experience on which to base decisions for a larger, expanded programme.

Pilot programmes have several advantages. Technical and extension activities can be developed more easily on a small scale. Large commitments of funds, time, equipment and materials can be avoided until an effective approach is developed. The establishment of a strong partnership with a small number of individual villages provides the opportunity to develop solutions in close co-operation with the community.

:Jan Davis/Oxfam

Northern Ghana. The secretary of the community's Water and Health Committee discussing a project proposal with the people of Wunzugutinga.

Small-scale pilot programmes can have a wide demonstration effect by stimulating interest in other communities in the programme area who are not yet committed to becoming involved. Small-scale programmes are often termed 'demonstration projects' for this reason. Developing a pilot programme into a larger-scale, district-wide programme follows a natural progression. This is especially so in the training and development of staff. A small core of staff, after some experience, will themselves act as trainers, in a multiplying effect.

Whose proposal?

The degree to which the community can be directly involved in the drawing up of a proposal will depend on the scale of the programme. In a small-scale programme involving one community project, community representatives will usually draw up a proposal with the advice of the agency, if necessary.

For larger programmes, the support agency will draw up a proposal based on the information and views gathered during the preliminary planning stage. The important factor must be the extent to which the community have been able to contribute to the process.

It is worth remembering that an agency engineer, a government administrator, a community leader, a farmer, and a woman water collector will all have their own, possibly different, views of a programme and what it should aim to achieve.

Clearly, the representatives of the community, the agency and the government, where appropriate, should all agree on the proposal before a programme moves ahead.

4.2 The written proposal

The written proposal needs to be in a form which can be understood by a wide range of people — community representatives, government officials, agency staff and donors. It should contain all the relevant facts necessary for decisions to be taken on whether to go ahead and fund the programme. Proposals should try to:

* be brief and to the point;
* use clear language;
* include all the key facts;
* indicate the sources of information;

- indicate a clear plan for the duration of the programme.

The agency may fund the programme itself or it may need to look for external donors to support the programme. The proposal must therefore put forward a clear case to the agency decision makers and potential funders for support of the programme. A programme proposal will normally include:

- Background: a brief history of the programme and how it arose.
- Justification: why the programme is a good idea.
- Objectives: the benefits to be achieved.
- Outputs: the targets set to achieve the objectives.
- Activities: how the targets will be achieved.
- Timeframe: a proposed start date and important dates in the programme, with a completion date.
- Gender impact statement: how women will benefit.
- Staffing: who, how many, and to do what
- Training: who will be trained and in what; who will do the training.
- Budget: what the money will be spent on and when.
- Monitoring: how the programme will be monitored
- Evaluation: when the programme will be evaluated.

Objectives, outputs, and activities

Community water supply programmes will have health, social, and/or economic benefits. There is a need to be more specific about how these benefits will be achieved by stating clear objectives, outputs, and activities.

Objectives

Programme objectives are the benefits to be achieved. For example, these could include:

- reduction in skin and eye diseases;
- reduction in the incidence of diarrhoea;
- reduction in the incidence of guinea-worm disease;
- reduction in women's workloads related to carrying water.

Outputs

Programme outputs correspond to the targets necessary to achieve the objectives. So, to achieve the above, the following targets might be set:

- Increase the amount of water available for face and body washing so that, at the end of the dry season, the average quantity of water available will be 24 litres per person per day (24 l/p/d).

- Increase knowledge and awareness of water-washed diseases such that 70 per cent of randomly selected adults understand the importance of hand-washing to prevent the transmission of diarrhoea.

- Increase knowledge and awareness of the transmission of guinea-worm disease so that 80 per cent of randomly selected adults understand the need to filter water from an open source through a filter cloth before drinking.

- Decrease the average distance a woman must walk to a source of water to a maximum of 250 metres from any village household.

Activities

Programme activities are the detailed actions required to achieve the programme outputs. So, for the above outputs, the following activities might be recommended:

- Each new well should be designed to serve 300 people. It should have sufficient yield of water at the end of the dry season to recharge overnight and supply 24 litres per person per day.

- Hygiene education activities will include individual and group meetings with women, men and children on the value of hand-washing to prevent the transmission of diarrhoea.

- Hygiene education activities will include slide film presentations on guinea-worm disease in villages followed by practical group demonstrations of filtering water. The programme will promote the sale of filter cloth.

- 50 new wells will be constructed such that each household will be within a distance of 250 metres of a well.

Setting out the objectives, outputs and activities in this way acts as a focus for the whole programme. Detailed planning will refine the outputs and activities, and their timing. Monitoring will show whether the activities are progressing as planned, and if the outputs are being achieved.

Continuing the previous example, 50 wells may be constructed in a programme but will they continue to function? If they continue functioning, will they be used by the community? A programme fails if the improved supplies break down or people do not use them. Therefore, further outputs which relate to both the *functioning* and *use* of a supply should be included. These outputs act as a guide for monitoring and evaluation:

- One year after construction, each well shall continue to supply safe drinking water at the original design rate of 24 l/p/d.

- All improved supplies shall be used by 70 per cent of the original target group of intended beneficiaries at the end of the first year, and 90 per cent in subsequent years.

Timeframe and targets

A proposal needs to provide a reliable estimate of targets and the timeframe required to achieve them. It also has to be flexible enough to allow for the realistic participation of communities, especially in the detailed planning phase. In setting a target of projects to be completed, it is better to aim for a smaller number of good quality projects rather than a larger number of poor quality projects.

Too high a target can raise people's expectations. If it is not met, then disappointment may follow. This can also lead to loss of confidence and interest in a programme. It is easier to start with a low target and build up a programme slowly as approaches and techniques are developed through experience.

Too low a target may not be cost-effective, and funding will be difficult to attract. A measure of the numbers of wells completed is still important, but should be viewed within the framework of a community-agency partnership in which the time allocated is sufficient for maximum community involvement. A programme's pace should reflect the needs of the community, not the wishes of the agency. Consideration should also be given to the quality of the finished work, and not just the number of wells completed.

When setting targets, agencies should not only consider the numbers of new supplies completed, but the percentage of supplies still working after a number of years. The emphasis should be on whether the supplies continue to function and be used.

Gender impact statement

Most proposals to NGO, bilateral, and multilateral agencies usually include a gender impact statement. That is, the programme background should indicate how women will be involved in the programme and how they will benefit from it. Agencies ask for this statement because of the way in which women have been ignored in the past.

The Oxfam Project Application Summary Form, which is used when applying to Oxfam for funds, includes the following requirements in the section headed 'Project Description':

- Project background, including details of consultation with women and men in the local community.

- How will this project help poor women and men of the local community?

- How will this project affect the status and workload of women? What is their role in decision making?

Asking for a gender impact statement helps to ensure that women's interests are considered in the formulation of a programme.

Staffing and training

The number and type of staff who are going to be involved in the programme should be outlined. Job descriptions of the main posts, indicating their responsibilities, could be included with a description of the type of persons suited to the jobs — person specifications. A simple staff organisation diagram should show how staff relate to each other and interact with other organisations and the community.

If the programme proposes the training of staff, either from the agency, the government, or the community, then the type and duration of the training should be outlined in the proposal. If regular training and workshops are going to be held there should be a plan and budget for these. Provision for outside trainers and training materials should be made.

Budget

An estimate of the total funds needed to implement the programme will be required by an agency and donor. This is the programme budget.

A budget estimate is usually required before the detailed planning and project design can be completed with each individual community. This is a particular problem in community water supply programmes. A solution might be to introduce two stages of funding:

- the first stage of funding, for detailed planning;
- the second stage of funding, for implementation.

However, in practice, the two phases are not so clear cut. Detailed planning will involve extended consultation with each community. Extension activities and hygiene education will be taking place in some communities at the same time as the construction of improved supplies will be taking place in other communities. The different stages and activities are integrated. (See the programme cycle bar chart on page 58).

Estimates will have to be based on information gathered during the preliminary planning stage. Only after the first year or two will it be possible to judge the accuracy of the estimates. There is, therefore, a case for financing a programme for an initial period only, with the intention of reassessing the funding after some experience. The attraction of a pilot programme is that initial funds can be allocated for small-scale activities on which to base more accurate funding for an expanded programme.

A budget is normally split into several components, which combine to give a total programme cost:

The manager of a hand-dug wells programme in Wolayta, Ethiopia submitted a budget with the following components for each financial year:

- *Salaries and subsistence: including gross annual salary of all contract staff, a percentage rise each year for inflation and increments, living expenses for staff outside their contract base, and casual labour.*

- *Vehicle maintenance and fuel: average annual running costs for different types of vehicle in the fleet including trucks, a four-wheel drive vehicle and bicycles, based on the estimated number of kilometres that would be travelled, and fuel consumption per kilometre.*

- *Capital equipment: tipper truck, motorcycles, bicycles, tripods, ring moulds, dewatering pumps, and camping equipment.*

- *Construction materials: cement, sand, stone, aggregate, reinforcement, including the cost of transporting the materials to the site.*

Monitoring and evaluation

The proposal should indicate how the programme will be monitored and who will do the monitoring. Monitoring provides some of the information required for the evaluation process. Evaluation will assess programme performance by comparing the initial objectives and outputs, as stated in the proposal, with the actual achievements. Evaluation is considered in more detail in Chapter 7.

Evaluations can take place at any time. However, they commonly take place mid-term and at the end of the programme. The advantages of planning evaluations at the beginning of a programme are that they are definitely included at the outset and not added as an afterthought; and funds can be allocated in advance to ensure the evaluations have enough financial support to be carried out well.

4.3 Guidelines and agreements

Guidelines

Some governments provide guidelines for the co-ordination of activities in the water and sanitation sector, with which agencies are asked to comply. Guidelines are often specifically aimed at NGOs:

> *One of the reasons the Ghana Water and Sewerage Corporation (GWSC) gave for issuing their guidelines was because of 'confusion between beneficiary communities due to disparities in the approach of different NGOs and lack of guaranteed maintenance of systems'.*

Guidelines can help to standardise approaches, where appropriate:

> *To avoid the situation where some villages paid a contribution for handpump maintenance and others did not, the GWSC established a sum to be paid by each village for every handpump installed. The guidelines explained, 'the fund set up by the contribution shall be kept in a special account, under control of the programme administration, or under control of the community itself. All NGOs are obliged to comply to ensure uniformity.'*

Guidelines concerning technology can encourage standardisation and assist long-term maintenance:

> *In the past, many organisations in Ethiopia installed handpumps of their own choice, resulting in a wide variety of handpump types throughout the country. This made it extremely difficult for the gov-*

ernment agency responsible for maintenance to repair and maintain them all. Therefore, the Water Resources Commission announced that only the Afridev handpump should be installed on boreholes or shallow wells for pumping depths between 10 and 45 metres.

Standardisation of equipment such as handpumps can help in long-term maintenance because tools, spare parts and training can also be standardised.

The aims of guidelines for NGOs and other agencies working in the water and sanitation sector can be summarised as follows:

- to inform agencies of their legal obligations;

- to set out the government's policy for the water and sanitation sector;

- to maintain adequate construction and equipment standards;

- to ensure appropriate technology is used;

- to recommend standard community contributions;

- to ensure adequate provision for operation and maintenance through sufficient funding, training and the provision of spare parts.

Agency-government agreements

Most NGOs negotiate aid agreements with the host government on the commencement of the NGO's country programme. These agreements cover the agency's general development work within the country. Additional agreements for operational programmes may also be required, where appropriate, with the relevant government agency. A proposal can form the basis of an agreement.

The typical responsibilities and obligations that could be included in a community water programme agreement between a government water agency and an NGO are illustrated in the following extracts taken from an NGO agreement with the Ethiopian Water Supply and Sewerage Authority (WSSA).

Responsibilities and obligations of WSSA:

- Co-ordinate the activities of the programme with other similar activities in the region.

- Approve designs and specifications.

- Inspect each of the wells constructed under the programme and certify satisfactory completion.

- Undertake responsibility for major repairs to handpumps installed under the programme, the repair of which is beyond the capability of local handpump caretakers.

- Take over handpump spare parts to be supplied by the NGO and supply them, under the system agreed, to water committees on a cost basis for the repair of handpumps.

- Arrange for the secondment of a trainer of extension agents and technical advisers, respectively, to be attached to the programme.

- Arrange with the Ministry of Health for the training of the programme community health educators.

Responsibilities and obligations of the NGO:

- Undertake to establish water management committees.

- Undertake health and hygiene education activities on water-related diseases with advice from the Ministry of Health.

- Supervise the construction of 70 hand dug wells and 20 protected springs.

- Fund all the equipment, vehicles, tools and materials necessary for the construction programme.

- Submit the final designs and specification of wells and springs to the water authority for approval.

- Employ and train staff for programme activities at the agency's own expense.

- Comply with the prevailing labour laws.

- Provide to the water authority all spares sufficient for five years' operation of the installed handpumps.

- Submit quarterly progress reports to the water authority and an annual report at the end of the dry season.

- Submit a programme completion report at the end of the programme.

The signing of an agreement between agency and government should be to the advantage of the communities who are to benefit from the programme. The agreement confirms the commitment of the relevant government agency to long-term back-up of the improved water supplies. It also approves the actions of the agency and therefore helps to safeguard the community from inappropriate programmes.

Checklist of questions

- Was the community involved in the drawing up of your programme proposal?

- Did community representatives approve the programme before it began?

- Do government guidelines exist that your agency should be following?

- Does a formal written agreement exist between your agency and the government? If not, would a formal agreement help the long-term success of the programme?

Further reading

Eade, D. and Williams, S. (editors) (forthcoming), *The Oxfam Handbook for Development Workers*, Oxford: Oxfam. (This is a completely revised edition of the book formerly known as *The Field Directors' Handbook*.)

5

Implementing projects

The implementation of a programme will involve the management of several integrated components. Individual projects will require further detailed planning with each community. This chapter considers how these various activities can be successfully implemented.

5.1 The integration of components

An integrated community water supply programme will include a combination of the following components:

- community/agency liaison

- hygiene education

- water supply development

- sanitation improvements.

Each component will have its own activities, staff, methods of working, and time scale. To be effective, the components need to be integrated so that their activities coincide and support each other. For example, hygiene education on the need to use more water for washing will be more effective if, at the same time, more water is made available through improvements to existing water sources.

Community liaison staff, also known as extension workers, provide the link between the community, educators, and the technical team. The same staff may have both extension and hygiene education responsibilities:

The Water Supply and Sewerage Authority (WSSA) in Ethiopia, employ Community Participation Promotion Agents (CPPAs) whose task is to act as a link between the community and the water authority. The CPPAs' training includes water supply and sanitation technologies, health and hygiene education, and communication methods. They carry out hygiene education prior to, during, and after water supply improvements.

The time scale required for the implementation of each component can vary considerably. Water supply improvements may be completed within one dry season. The development of effective community water supply management, however, may take considerably longer. Sanitation improvements and changes in hygiene behaviour are likely to take several years.

Sanitation improvements are normally not as immediately attractive as a better water supply. Therefore, more time is often required to 'sell' the idea of improving sanitation than is required to gain support for water supply improvements.

The approach to water supply and sanitation improvements will not be the same. A water system will supply a community. It will be communally owned and managed. Sanitation improvements will usually be at the household level. This requires a different approach from the construction of a communal water system because decisions and improvements will take place at the household level, not at the community level.

Hygiene promotion through education plays a major role in the encouragement of better sanitation and the hygienic care and use of a water supply. All the components need to be carefully integrated.

5.2 Hygiene education

The terms 'health education' and 'hygiene education' are often used loosely. Both terms occur in this book. Hygiene education is part of health education but is specifically about encouraging people to adopt clean practices to prevent illness. However, even if people are aware of safe hygiene practices they may not be in a position to follow them due to a range of constraints.

Hygiene education, then, should be seen as a part of hygiene promotion which looks at removing the constraints to safe hygienic practices, such as a lack of water and sanitation facilities, in an integrated way with the other components of a water supply programme.

Hygiene education messages

Education includes the passing on of advice, information and ideas. A way of passing on information with impact is through a short, simple message that is readily remembered. What are the hygiene education messages that, according to each community, may need to be passed on?

Hygiene messages may be grouped under three categories: personal hygiene, household hygiene, and community hygiene:

Personal hygiene messages can be based on the following advice:

- Wash hands regularly, and always before preparing or eating food, with soap or ash if possible.

- Bathe regularly.

- Use a latrine, if available.

- Wash children regularly.

- Wash clothes and bedding regularly.

- Use a clean vessel for drinking water.

Household hygiene messages can be based on the following advice:

- Keep animals out of living areas.

- Use a safe method of excreta disposal.

- Keep a designated area for the disposal of waste water and household solid waste.

- Dispose of waste by burning or burying it.

- Clean household utensils regularly.

- Ensure the safe and hygienic storage of food, water and cooking equipment.

- Clean the house regularly.

- Keep flies and insects off food and water.

- Keep water storage pots covered.

Community hygiene messages can be based on the following advice:

- Keep the areas around water sources well-drained and clean.

- Provide clean communal toilets at markets, bars, restaurants, churches and mosques.

• Keep animals away from waterpoints and latrines.

• Keep footpaths and roads free from rubbish and human waste.

• Provide a safe means of disposing of waste water and solid waste from public places such as markets.

Putting the messages across

Hygiene educators can use a variety of methods including:

• Demonstrations

• Lecturing

• Discussion

• Posters and pamphlets

• Slides, films and videos

• Drama and puppets

• Role play and story-telling

There is also education potential through the mass media: newspapers, radio, and television.

The way in which these methods can be used and combined is illustrated by a case study from northern Ghana:

Across the Upper Regions of Ghana 2,600 boreholes were drilled and fitted with handpumps by the Ghana Water and Sewerage Corporation (GWSC), assisted by a bilateral agency. The main objective of this programme was to bring a safe, reliable water supply to within easy reach of households, and to reduce the incidence of guinea-worm disease among the region's one million inhabitants.

A few years later, an evaluation revealed that the incidence of guinea-worm disease had not markedly decreased. A health education component was then included in the programme. Training courses and workshops were organised for health professionals and extension agents employed by both the government and NGOs. At the same time, Village Health Workers (VHWs) were given training in two main topics:

• *how to avoid getting guinea-worm disease;*

• *the prevention and control of diarrhoea.*

The VHWs returned to their villages and organised meetings to pass on the information about guinea-worm and diarrhoea. As well as talking to groups and individuals, they also used drama and puppets to get the messages across.

The few villages with trained VHWs were able to benefit from the hygiene education. However, the question was how to reach a much wider audience. It was fortunate that at this time an FM radio station was starting to broadcast in the region:

An agreement was reached with the Ghana Broadcasting Corporation to put out health education programmes which would reach thousands of people in the region. First, a Radio Learning Group (RLG) was formed in a few pilot communities. Each group was given a transistor radio which was only capable of receiving the FM station. They were also given a manual which supported the messages transmitted by the programme.

A series of programmes on the health and hygiene aspects of water and sanitation were produced. The leader of the RLG would invite people to listen to the broadcasts and then have a discussion, with the aid of the manual, on what they had just heard.

Eventually, all 2,600 communities with handpumps had a Radio Learning Group. Programmes are now broadcast in the six languages of the region.

Monitoring of the effectiveness of the health education indicated reductions in the incidence of guinea-worm disease. Radio proved to be an effective medium for health education for the following reasons:

- Quality messages were produced and passed on in a consistent, organised and entertaining way.

- People liked listening to the radio.

- The programmes generated a lot of discussion which, with the use of the manual, reinforced the messages.

- There was an opportunity for groups to respond to the messages by writing in to the programme.

Through these broadcasts, improved hygiene and sanitation practices were brought to public awareness in a way that had not happened before.

The original water programme did not achieve its aim of reducing the incidence of guinea-worm because it did not integrate a health and hygiene education component with the borehole drilling activities. The education component was only brought in later, to achieve the original aim. This example clearly shows the importance of integrating the different components of water supply improvements and health education, from the very beginning of a programme.

Educational video films can be a usful way of getting messages across:

The Department of Community Development toured villages in northern Ghana showing a video film on the causes of river blindness disease. It showed how to recognise the early signs of the disease and what to do when it was identified. It gave an opportunity to explain the river blindness eradication programme so that people understood the disease prevention activities being undertaken in the region.

Educational video films can have a big impact if used in an appropriate way and adapted to local circumstances. However, in countries where many different languages are spoken it would be difficult and expensive to produce videos in all the languages. In the above example, a local interpreter, such as a schoolteacher, had to be found, to interpret the English soundtrack into the local language. This was clearly unsatisfactory.

When should hygiene education take place?

Hygiene education is appropriate at every stage in the programme cycle. (See the programme cycle bar chart on p.58).

- During the planning stage before construction — to motivate interest and provide information on why an improved water supply or method of sanitation is important.

- During construction — to build on earlier hygiene education, to relate the messages to the improvements being made, and to prepare the community for the hygienic use and management of the new facilities.

- After construction — to reinforce the messages and to guide the initial use and management of the facilities.

An example of poorly prepared hygiene education taking place before the start of construction is seen in this case study from southern Ethiopia:

Meetings were addressed at each village visited by a health education unit. Hygiene education consisted of two lectures on various aspects of hygiene related to water and sanitation. Three films were shown in

113

the evenings. Unfortunately, the films were not in the local language so an extension agent talked over the soundtrack. The films were only shown once, though it was probable that this was the first time the communities had ever seen a film. The indications were that the people were more interested in the video equipment than the health message in the film.

There are important points to be made about this particular case:

- The unit came from the capital so they were not familiar with the local culture or language.

- The unit had not allowed any time to get to know the villagers or their specific health problems.

- The unit's programme was a few months ahead of construction so it was likely that people would have forgotten some of the messages by the time the handpumps and latrines were built.

The lessons to be learnt from this example are:

- Try to use materials produced in the local language.

- Do not make assumptions about people's health problems.

- Co-ordinate hygiene education activities with other components of the programme so that the messages have maximum impact.

Sometimes specific hygiene education topics are most effectively dealt with at certain times of the year. This is because some health problems show a seasonal variation. For example, cases of malaria and diarrhoea may both peak at the beginning of the wet season. Other diseases can show seasonal patterns:

In northern Ghana, guinea-worm disease peaked just as farmers were beginning to prepare their land. The disease has almost a 12-month cycle, from drinking contaminated water to the emergence of a worm from the skin. Therefore, education on the value of filtering unsafe water was concentrated during the dry season, just before planting, at the time when people are at highest risk of contracting the disease. The importance of filtering the water, or using protected well water, was emphasised by the many crippling cases to be seen at that time of the year.

Education about guinea-worm disease was timed to have the greatest effect when the disease was at its most severe and when people were at highest risk.

Where should hygiene education take place?

Gerry Garvey/Oxfam

Wollo, Ethiopia. Careful selection of hygene education material is necessary.

In Wolayta, Ethiopia, follow-up hygiene education took place at the well site:

> *Extension agents arranged for groups of neighbouring households to come to the well for training in how to use the handpump correctly, and how to keep the drainage apron clean. The session was also used to reinforce the health benefits of collecting more water and using it for more frequent body washing.*

Hygiene education at the well site can help to reinforce the potential health benefits of an improved water supply. However, sufficient staff must be available to hold enough meetings to reach more than a fraction of the population:

> *In Ethiopia, a health educator used a set of flip charts in sessions limited to groups of 30 people. This enabled everyone to see the charts. However, the programme manager soon realised that the time and staff required to meet with everyone in a large village of several hundred people had been seriously under-estimated. With a target of*

50 new wells a year, it became clear that the health education component could never keep pace with the well construction rate.

The health education components of many water programmes are simply added in by planners who do not realise the amount of time and number of specialised staff required for the effective implementation of a health and hygiene education programme.

To multiply the effectiveness of programme staff, trained members of the community can act as promoters of hygiene education messages, as in the earlier example of trained village health workers.

Health education aids

General health and hygiene education materials are often made available through aid organisations and networking centres. These can include slide films with taped commentaries, flip charts, and more recently, videos. The problem with this type of material is their general nature. The need for translation may reduce their effectiveness. Viewers might find it difficult to identify with pictures from another culture:

FILTER YOUR DRINKING WATER

Tamale, Ghana. Slides, charts, and posters can give a direct health message

116

A bilateral agency funded the development of a set of hygiene education flipcharts based on scenes from the daily life of a Muslim pastoralist community in southern Ethiopia. A small-scale NGO water programme working with Christian farming communities adopted the flipchart set for use in their own hygiene education work in northern Ethiopia. However, it was not successful, because the Christian farmers could not relate their daily life to that of the Muslim pastoralists, as the two cultures were so different.

Appropriate slide shows can be effective in village meetings as in the following situation in northern Ghana:

Slide shows on the prevention of guinea-worm disease were held in the open air during the evening. Extension staff showed the slides on a large screen erected on a vehicle. Power for the slide projector came from the vehicle battery. The presenters tried not to talk too much but asked questions about each picture to encourage discussion. The slides were taken in the village of a neighbouring tribal group across the border in Togo. People looked familiar, they wore similar clothing, and the slides showed recognisable scenes. Viewers were able to relate to the pictures.

Jan Davis/Oxfam

Kubagna, Ghana. Practical demonstrations can reinforce a health message.

Flip-chart and slide-show health education can be followed up by practical demonstrations to reinforce the message:

The day after a slide-show evening, extension staff visited households within the village. These visits included demonstrations to reinforce and build on what had been seen the previous evening.

5.3 Sanitation

A common form of improved sanitation is the pit latrine. There are a number of factors which determine the appropriateness and effectiveness of pit latrines. Technical factors include:

- Soil conditions — hard rock or collapsing soils will make it difficult or dangerous to dig a pit.

- Groundwater table — a high water table will flood a pit which can lead to smells and the breeding of mosquitoes.

- Location — latrines must be located at a safe distance downhill from wells and springs to prevent the contamination of drinking water.

Jan Davis

Damazin, Sudan. The use of local materials can keep the cost of a household latrine at an affordable level.

- The design of latrine — a simple pit or ventilated pit; for squatting or seated position; related to the type of anal cleansing materials used.

- Building materials and skills — the use of local materials and skills for maintenance and the ease of copying the design.

Social and economic factors include:

- Local customs and beliefs related to excreta.

- The knowledge and awareness of individuals concerning excreta disposal.

- The level of interest and motivation for improved sanitation.

- The acceptance of individual, family or communal latrines.

- The cost of improved sanitation.

Reference should be made to the sanitation publications listed at the end of this chapter for detailed consideration of the above issues

Creating a demand for latrines

Constructing latrines does not automatically mean they will be used and maintained. A better approach is to first of all create a demand for latrines through an education programme:

In the Zezencho area of southern Ethiopia, an agency held meetings at which slides were shown to illustrate talks on good sanitation and hygiene practices, and to introduce the concept of pit latrines. The agency did not build any latrines, but responded to requests from the local kebele (village council) for help in organising sanitation committees. The committees, each of four women, organised the construction of household latrines in their villages. It was up to each individual household to dig its pit. Artisans in the village were then trained by agency staff to complete the latrines. Once trained, these artisans helped other villagers to build latrines. Because the latrines were affordable and did not require any outside building materials, the idea of having a latrine soon spread. A pit latrine became a status symbol. Now most households have, and use, a pit latrine.

The crucial factor here was that the building of latrines was not imposed from outside. Instead, appropriate hygiene education and demonstration latrines stimulated demand for affordable latrines. The two components of a programme, hygiene education and the support of

119

sanitation improvements, need to be closely integrated if a programme is to be successful.

5.4 Construction supervision

The following section considers the supervision of community construction activities. There are important differences between the supervision of a directly employed workforce and an unskilled, perhaps voluntary, community workforce.

Work may be interrupted by market days, weddings, funerals, and so on. Unskilled farmers working only one day in a week on a rota basis will need more careful supervision than permanently employed staff who get to know a job well by working every day.

There are therefore important issues to consider concerning the timing and organisation of work, the quality of construction, and safety.

When should construction work take place?

Construction work must fit into a community's seasonal pattern of activities:

> *During the dry season in northern Ghana, people were able to find time to work on communal projects. The scarcity of water at this time of the year provided an immediate incentive for the improvement of water supplies. Projects needed to be finished by the end of the dry season before farmers were drawn back to their fields, and the rains made construction work impossible again.*

It is difficult, or even impossible, in some climates to proceed with construction work during the rainy season. Farmers will be busy during this season, but they can still make decisions about the coming construction work, carry out routine maintenance, and take part in hygiene education meetings.

Voluntary work

Voluntary community labour has often been regarded by outsiders as free labour. But people's time also has value. As an alternative to community work people might spend more time on productive farming activities, for example. Agency staff should not make assumptions about the time people have available for 'community work'.

Agencies should also be aware that people's time can be 'volunteered' by others. Community leaders may give assurances that 'everybody wants water so everybody will come out to work' without really consulting 'everybody' first. Men in leadership positions may 'volunteer' women for work without the women having much say in the matter. Agencies should ensure that volunteer labour has not been coerced in some way by village or political leaders.

Good supervision is especially important in work involving volunteers. A manager is ultimately responsible for the safety and standard of work and should therefore direct the work in a way which ensures close supervision by staff.

Guidelines are required to make clear the division of responsibilities between extension and technical staff. Arrangements need to be made for work rota organisation, weekly work plans, the supply of tools, food for the workers, and so on:

The Community Participation Promotion Agents (CPPAs) in Ethiopia were responsible for establishing water committees in villages. Each committee acted as a link between community, extension, and construction staff, and appointed a number of representatives with responsibility for community organisation during the construction phase of work. In practice, the CPPAs spent considerable periods of time at some projects. Piped supplies, for example, required extensive community organisation for trench digging.

Compromises will always need to be made between the best technical approach and the most acceptable approach:

In the village of La-atarigu, northern Ghana, a team of six farmers arrived each morning to dig a well under the direction of two supervisors. The rota for each team meant that it would work one day every seven days. Each team worked a different day. All the farmers were happy with this arrangement as it allowed them to work on their farms for six days of the week.

However, the work would have been easier to supervise with a fixed well-digging team, as training would only have to be given to one team rather than to many different people. Extension agents suggested the fixed team approach to the village chief but it was rejected. The fixed team approach meant that the members of the team would have to be given some compensation for the time lost working on their farms. The membership of the team and the compensation could not be agreed and the rota system was accepted instead.

Quality and standards

A manager has to ensure that agreed work procedures are followed by construction staff, and that the quality of work reaches a certain standard:

A manager was on a site visit to the village of Wunzugutinga in northern Ghana to inspect the progress of well lining using pre-cast concrete rings. A concrete ring was being rolled into position when it cracked and collapsed. On investigation, the manager discovered the sand used was not of the required quality, and the concrete had not been mixed correctly. The inspection, and a change in procedure, prevented any further collapsing rings.

It is the responsibility of managers to ensure that correct procedures are followed on site so that an acceptable standard of work is maintained.

A manager has an important role in the interpretation of technical drawings for those who cannot read them. Without the necessary background and training it is not easy for people to visualise what an object looks like from a drawing. Models can be used in place of drawings. For example, they can be used to great effect to explain the process of digging and lining a well. Technical drawings may be necessary for the discussion and presentation of ideas between engineers but models and practical demonstrations are usually more effective on site.

Kubore, Ghana. The regular inspection and checking of work are important.

Gerry Garvey/Oxfam

Wolayta, Ethiopia. Design drawings need to be explained carefully to site staff.

Safety

The staff and community workers have a responsibility to each other for personal safety but it is the manager who is ultimately responsible for the safety of all the people involved in programme activities. Close supervision is part of ensuring safe practices.

The public must be considered. Spectators and animals should be controlled and kept away from work sites. A site must be protected and not left overnight in a dangerous condition. Safety procedures should be covered in staff training, and reviewed in the light of experience. Guidelines can be established for specific types of work.

To quote the Oxfam technical manual *Safety in Wells*:

'It is of paramount importance that all reasonable precautions are taken to ensure that what is intended to be a life saving project, the provision of good water supplies, does not cause tragic loss of life or limb through ignorance or carelessness during construction or maintenance operations.'

Many people are not aware of the dangers in construction work:

An integrated rural development programme in Sudan became involved in hand dug well construction for the first time. The

123

inexperienced staff used a small diesel-engine-powered centrifugal pump for dewatering. While digging the first seven metres, the pump was kept on the surface some distance from the well, with a suction hose lowered into the water. This method was quite safe, as the carbon monoxide exhaust gas from the engine did not enter the well excavation.

As the digging continued, like all suction pumps, the pump was not able to lift water from below seven metres depth. The crew decided to lower the engine down the side of the well, suspended on a rope. As digging continued, the exhaust fumes circulated around the excavation and settled to the bottom of the well. Within seconds the two diggers at the bottom of the well collapsed, dead.

There are several safe methods of dewatering wells which can be used below a depth of seven metres. Programme managers have a responsibility to ensure that safe working practices are known and followed at all times.

Northern Ghana. Air-operated pumps provide a safe method of dewatering a well.

5.5 Monitoring and reporting

Monitoring and reporting can be divided between activities relating to the implementation of a programme (which are considered in this chapter);

124

and activities relating to the management of a completed water supply (which are considered in Chapter 6).

Monitoring and evaluation

Monitoring and evaluation are closely related. *Monitoring* is the process of collecting information on programme activities. *Evaluation* uses the monitoring information to assess programme progress. Monitoring is a regular activity which continues throughout the life of a programme. (See the programme cycle bar chart on page 58.) The information gathered through monitoring, together with the baseline information gathered during the planning stage, is essential for any future overall programme evaluation. The evaluation of a programme is considered separately in the final chapter.

The community's involvement in the monitoring process helps everyone to understand the difficulties and contribute to the solutions. Community involvement in monitoring assists in the preparation of the community for the full management of their water supply on completion.

It is important to monitor health and hygiene education to assess their impact:

The Water and Education For Health (WEFH) unit in northern Ghana,which was supported by a bilateral agency, assessed the impact of their educational campaigns by monitoring and evaluating specific activities. In their initial campaign, the impact of educational meetings was assessed.

People taking part in the survey were asked to answer the same questionnaire before the campaign, and after the campaign. This allowed for a measurement of what people had learned from the educational messages put across in the meetings.

The information which is useful to programme implementers and designers is whether people are interested in the activities, and how they respond. Hygiene education monitoring will want to find out:

* How many people attend meetings.

* Who attends education sessions: women, men, children.

* What additional knowledge people have gained.

* If messages are being understood or misunderstood.

The amount and kind of knowledge gained may be discovered by monitoring before, and after a campaign. The results are then compared.

Extension workers can find out:

- The number of additional questions people can answer on a questionnaire.

- The change in the percentage of people who can demonstrate particular activities; for example, mothers who correctly prepare oral rehydration solution.

- If there are any signs of changes in behaviour, for example, the number of households where the water pots are covered.

Time must be allowed for people to adjust their behaviour permanently in response to an educational programme. It is important not to monitor too early.

Public reaction to education activities can itself be a useful monitoring indicator:

Following a series of village meetings about guinea-worm disease prevention in northern Ghana, a health educator received many requests to purchase filter cloths. She decided to sell suitable cloth for filtering water during field visits. As each cloth was sold, she noted the village where the buyer came from. After a period of time, the figures indicated the villages where the particular health message on the need to filter water was having greatest impact.

Recording of project information

There is a lot of information which could be gathered for monitoring purposes but how often is it recorded? The recording of project data is sometimes seen as a tiring burden, and so people give it little attention, as the following situation from Ethiopia shows:

A programme manager was not very interested in paper work. Written records of the first year's construction were poor, and the cause of some embarrassment. People frequently asked questions such as 'How deep is this well? How many bags of cement did you use? How much money did this improvement cost? What proportion of the total cost was spent on materials?' The manager could not answer their questions because no records had been kept.

A poor excuse often given for the failure to record construction data is that there is no time. A simple system, however, can easily be set up for supervisors to follow, which does not take much time and can save a lot of time in the long term. Notes should be taken at the time of construction, before information is forgotten.

It benefits all programme staff to keep good records:

The same manager slowly began to realise the importance of recording data, and during the second year of the programme made a determined effort to ensure that staff collected and recorded field data. It was a pleasant surprise to find how this data, which had been recorded reluctantly, helped the manager in the planning of the third year of the programme. It also helped to answer all those questions people asked!

Factual data can be a great help in future planning. It should be possible to make more realistic estimates of:

- the number of projects which can be constructed;

- the amount of construction material, vehicle fuel, and labour required;

- the cost.

A programme manager's job can be made much easier by keeping good records. The collection and recording of data by field staff enables them to be more involved in monitoring and the future planning of a programme.

Materials and stock control

In a community water supply programme, delays on site due to a lack of materials can severely disappoint villagers who may have given up valuable farming time to make themselves available for work. Enthusiasm for a project can easily be lost due to delays.

Careful monitoring of tools, equipment and materials should ensure they are available and ready when needed:

In the rush to start implementing a new programme in Ethiopia, little consideration was given to the establishment of an effective stock control system. After some time it was realised that no inventory of stock was available, and nobody really knew what was or was not, in the store.

The implementation of a stock control system at the outset of the programme might have taken some time, but would have avoided many problems, and saved months of subsequent work getting records straight. It might also have prevented the theft of many tools and bags of cement, which was discovered later.

Gerry Garvey/Oxfam

Boditi, Ethiopia. Stock control is vital for accountability and efficient work.

Written reports

Written reports are a way of passing on information to those who want to know what is happening in a programme. Good monitoring makes reporting easier and reflects what is actually taking place and not what the report writer thinks is happening.

A manager needs to make time for report writing within a busy schedule of day-to-day activities. Report writing can be made easier by having an established framework for regular reports. For example, a set of subheadings can be established which will always be reported on: summary of activities, projects completed, new construction, programme staff, training, expenditure, and so on. This approach gives consistency to reports. It helps the reader to pinpoint information which also makes it useful when it comes to monitoring and evaluating a project.

Reports should be kept brief and to the point if they are to be read by busy people. The use of graphs and other diagrams can make a clear visual impact and can present information more clearly than putting it into words.

An NGO manager listed the following people and agencies requiring written reports:

- community representatives;

- programme staff;

- immediate manager;

- headquarters office through the manager;

- government agency with whom the programme had a national agreement;

- government water agency with whom the programme had a working agreement;

- government administrative and political bodies at district and regional level;

- other agencies working in the same geographical area.

The list indicates how much of a burden reporting can sometimes be. Some of the people and agencies could receive a copy of the same report. But some of the reports will contain different details, depending on what the readers want to know. For example, the immediate manager and head office will want accounting details, which will be of little interest to the water agency who will only want overall figures.

Battery power allows small laptop computers to be used in field offices. The ability to correct mistakes and edit material using a word processor aids the writing of reports. Other computer software can be used to assist stock control, the recording of project data, and in the production of accounts.

However, there are also drawbacks to the use of small laptop computers: an electricity supply is required for recharging batteries, dusty conditions can affect the electronics and keyboard, a suitable printer must be available, sufficient time and training must be provided for staff to learn the efficient use of both the hardware and software. A micro-computer is a useful tool but it should be remembered that the quality of reports depends on the writer, not the machine.

Financial and regular progress reports are required by funding agencies and donors as a minimum requirement for accountability. The reaction of a head office administrator in England on receiving a very poor field report from Ethiopia was the following:

'The donor has committed a lot of money to this programme and I think they deserve a bit more than one side of paper, four times a year. Your report doesn't even offer much qualitative or quantitative analysis. Knowing the work that is being done, all I can say is you are not doing yourselves justice in the reports. I am sure it is difficult to

appreciate the need for good reports when you are working away in the field, but it's one of those things, we can't fundraise without them!'

Funds are given by donors to support specific programmes. Donors expect to get reports on how the money is being spent. If they do not, then they will not give any more money. This is one reason why reports from the field must be regular and contain some basic information on progress.

It is especially important for small community groups to write good reports for their donors. This may be one of the few opportunities small groups have to communicate directly with their donors to inform them of the progress of a programme.

Community-agency reporting

Reporting between the community and agency may be through water committees, chiefs, or other community leaders. In most cases it will probably be a combination of verbal and written reporting:

At a meeting of village representatives in northern Ghana, the manager outlined a provisional programme for the coming year. Questions were asked, in particular about a proposed increase in cash contributions for starting a new well. The manager explained the effect on contributions of a high rise in the price of cement. After discussion, the level of the new contributions were agreed by the meeting. At the same meeting the community representatives gave a list of villages interested in the construction of new wells, to the programme manager.

Information sharing

There is a need for good liaison between all agencies working in the water and sanitation sector:

On updating their inventory of drinking-water supply projects, a Regional Office of the Ethiopian Water Supply and Sewerage Authority found little information on projects constructed by NGOs. It therefore sent a letter to all NGOs in the region, requesting basic information on the number of water projects and their location, type of pumping equipment, and so on. Unfortunately, the request met with a poor response. A few of the NGOs replied with detailed data, others provided general information, while most did not reply at all.

Some agencies have programme agreements directly with a water authority, and may be under an obligation to provide information. Others may not have an agreement but still report their activities to the authority. Preferably, all agencies should share basic information on their programmes to aid the co-ordination of activities.

Constructive information exchange is possible through workshops and conferences:

An Ethiopian water agency held a three-day conference every six months. Participants included agency staff, foreign aid organisations, donors, NGOs, and other interested parties. Each organisation presented their activities and specific approaches. Discussion followed in small workshop groups.

There is always a risk that programmes proceed without a full appreciation of the wider context in which they work. The kind of information exchange described above can help to place individual programmes in relation to the national situation. This is sure to help co-ordination. Interim workshops at a more local district or regional level can usefully supplement larger meetings.

5.6 Managing staff and vehicles

Recruitment of staff

What does a typical water programme personnel structure look like? Consider the following example from Ethiopia.

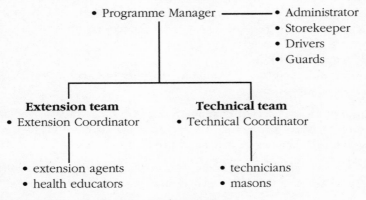

Figure 6 A typical personnel structure.

The responsibilities of each team in this programme were as follows:
The Extension Team:

- Baseline and follow-up socio-economic surveys.

- Formation of water committees and the training of committee members and caretakers.

- Hygiene education.

The Technical Team:

- Baseline and follow-up technical surveys.

- Construction of hand-dug wells and protected springs.

- Maintenance and repair of programme equipment.

It is helpful to write a job description for each member of staff. Job descriptions are important as they clarify the tasks and responsibilities of each person. The following is an example from Ethiopia:

Job title:	Programme Manager
Responsible to:	Agency Representative
Responsible for:	1 extension co-ordinator
	1 technical co-ordinator
	8 extension agents
	4 technicians
	4 masons
	2 drivers and 1 storekeeper
Location:	Wolayta, Ethiopia
Grade:	8 (on a scale of 1-10 for the country)
Job purpose:	To plan, manage, and implement the Wolayta Water Programme.

Specific responsibilities:
Manage the Wolayta Water Programme and personnel consisting of 20 staff and community members.

- Train and advise selected community members and project staff in methods of socio-economic and technical survey, design theory, construction techniques, and maintenance management.

- Work closely with the elected community water committees during the planning, implementation, and management phases of each project.

- Plan and implement each project in a participatory manner, especially with women's groups, so that women in particular benefit, as the main water users.

- Provide advice and support to hygiene education staff engaged in activities where water supply and sanitation improvements are planned.

- Establish monitoring and evaluation procedures for the regular assessment of all programme features.

- Liaise with relevant government agencies regarding rural water development in Wolayta

- Maintain budgetary and financial control in accordance with the agency's financial procedures.

- Prepare quarterly reports for submission to the agency and relevant government departments.

The recruitment of local staff

The policy of a rural community water programme in northern Ghana was to recruit and employ staff from within the programme area. The main advantages were:

- Local staff were motivated to assist in their own area.

- Skills were developed and remained in the community.

- Local knowledge was very useful in their work.

- There were no accommodation problems. Staff did not want leave to return to their home towns, as might staff recruited from outside the community.

The main disadvantages were:

- Few skills of the type required could be found locally.

- Additional time was required to train staff.

- Pressure was put on the manager to employ favoured individuals.

- Local politics more easily affected staff relations.

Despite the potential disadvantages, experience showed it was usually better to recruit staff from within the local communities rather than from outside.

Qualifications of senior field staff

The educational qualifications of a Community Participation Promotion Agent (CPPA) attached to the Wollo programme in Ethiopia were a completed school education and a nine-month diploma course in Community Development. The diploma course content included:

- basic rural economics;
- baseline community survey techniques;
- social aspects of rural water supply;
- technical aspects of rural water supply;
- water use patterns and popular perceptions;
- community participation;
- the role of popular organisations in development;
- development communication;
- water and health education;
- preventive maintenance;
- audio-visual equipment operation.

Recruitment of extension staff

In recruiting extension agents, the CPPA looked for people who met the following criteria:

- preferably a woman;
- a long-time resident of the programme area;
- a good communicator with village people;
- preferably an ability to read and write in the local language;
- prepared to travel on foot or on horseback, and live in different communities.

Extension work is a skilled job and requires a sensitive and understanding approach. Personal characteristics are, in many circumstances, more important than qualifications.

In practice, the criteria stated for the CPPA's extension agents may be difficult to meet in some societies. The two requirements of a preference for a woman and an ability to read and write may not be easily found together. Extensive education and training may be necessary.

In some societies, it is not realistic to expect to find a female extension agent who will be free to travel around the programme area on her own, staying in different villages. One way of enabling female extension agents to travel and spend nights away from home is to employ two women who can travel together.

Training of staff

Staff training can include: on-the-job training, courses, training workshops, and exchange visits.

On-the-job training takes place whilst carrying out regular work. The training requires competent supervisors to show how a job is done and to provide encouragement and advice to the trainees:

In a water project in northern Ghana, temporary supervisors were recruited from the project villages to work during the dry season construction period only. They had little knowledge of the skills required and therefore they had to be trained. A small team of permanent staff trained new temporary seasonal supervisors on-the-job. The necessary knowledge and skills were passed on by the permanent staff at each new stage of construction. At the end of the dry season the temporary supervisors returned to their farms. The more competent seasonal staff were employed again the following dry season.

On-the-job training must be carefully supervised for the work to be carried out safely and meet the standards required.

Training workshops can be a good environment for exchanging ideas and information:

In the Wollo Water Programme a two-day workshop was held for all staff members every six months. Each team within the programme gave a short presentation on a current aspect of their work. Each presentation was followed by questions and discussion. For example, the extension team would talk about the role and responsibilities of water committees, while the construction teams talked about problems they had faced in working with water committees. Through open discussion, the extension and technical staff began to appreciate each other's role in the programme, and to learn a great deal in the process.

Extension and technical staff often do not have a clear understanding of each other's roles, especially in the early stages of a programme. Regular training workshops can help understanding and promote good staff working relationships.

Short courses on a particular subject can be an effective way of learning a specific skill:

The Water Supply and Sewerage Authority (WSSA) regional office in southern Ethiopia held training courses for pump operators sponsored by an international NGO, who had constructed water supplies in several villages. The NGO paid daily allowances for the trainees and WSSA provided the training.

Short courses of a few days' to a few weeks' duration can benefit extension, technical, and administrative staff. It is important to match the needs of the individual with the skills level of the course.

Exchange visits provide an opportunity for staff to learn from other programmes:

In Ethiopia, the programme manager, extension and technical co-ordinators of a wells programme spent a week visiting similar programmes in another region of the country. They were able to discuss their own field experiences with people who had similar interests and experience. At one well site, the visitors were particularly impressed with the design of a headwall and drainage apron. They decided to experiment with a similar design on return to their own programme.

Exchange visits can be effective in stimulating new ideas. It is, however, important for an exchange to have clearly defined aims and objectives. This helps both parties to know what to expect of each other and to plan the exchange to meet the agreed aims and objectives. Exchange visits can be local, district to district, regional or inter-country.

Transport and vehicle maintenance

The importance of mobility in a water supply programme should not be underestimated. Reliable and serviceable vehicles are often essential to the operation of a programme. They can also be a significant item in a programme budget. Many programme managers are surprised at the amount of time and money which is required for vehicle maintenance:

A church-funded water programme in Bolosso, Ethiopia had two different types of Land Rover, and three different types of Toyota. The vehicles varied in age, up to 12 years old. They were maintained at a private garage in the nearby town. Repair and maintenance was very costly because all the spare parts were imported. A new model of vehicle was given by a foreign donor, but with no spare parts. The garage could only get the parts on the black market, at a very high price.

Awassa, Ethiopia. Motorcycles are often used by extension staff.

In this case, vehicle maintenance and fuel accounted for over 20 per cent of the programme budget. Standardisation would have helped to keep costs down:

The manager calculated the cost of employing a mechanic, setting up a workshop, and stocking spare parts. If all the vehicles had been of the same make and model then it would have been better to build a workshop than use a private garage. However, since the programme had six different vehicle models it was uneconomic for it to stock the quantity and variety of spares required to carry out its own maintenance. Standardisation of the vehicle fleet was going to take years to achieve. The programme therefore continued to pay high costs at the private garage.

Gerry Garvey/Oxfam

Alaba, Ethiopia. Bicycle maintenance is simple and cheap

The reason for such a variety of vehicles was that the small, church-based programme relied on several donors. They felt they could not afford to refuse the offer of a much needed vehicle in case they lost the chance of getting one at all. Donors need to be aware of the potential problems their donations sometimes create if these are not appropriate to local circumstances.

Initial programme proposals should specify vehicles common to the region and country in which they are to operate. Both the capital and running costs should be considered as a whole and alternatives compared. The availability of spare parts locally can make vehicle maintenance very much easier. Small programmes cannot hope to stock all the possible spares likely to be required.

If parts are not available locally, delays in water supply activities can be very serious and undermine a community's confidence in an agency.

If work sites are not widely scattered or the terrain is unsuitable for vehicles, bicycle or animal transport may be more appropriate:

A programme in northern Ghana employed centrally based supervisors who were issued with bicycles to visit work sites. The type of bicycle was very common throughout the country. Spare parts were available and there were cycle fitters at every major market. Running costs were very low.

Programmes should consider appropriate forms of transport for personnel, equipment and materials in rural areas.

Checklist of questions

- How does your programme integrate the different components of hygiene education, sanitation and water supply development?

- Do the staff of the different components meet and work with each other, or work separately?

- Does the present programme approach lead to coordinated action to improve the health of the community?

- In your programme, what are the main health and hygiene messages that need to be put across to the community?

- Are you using the most appropriate and effective methods to put across the hygiene education messages?

- How is hygiene education monitored in your programme?

- Is the training and supervision of members of the community sufficient to ensure safe working methods and an acceptable standard of work?

- Are sufficient records of activities kept to monitor progress and provide sufficient information for the future evaluation of the programme?

- Do your reports provide the information people really want to know? Are your reports too detailed or too brief?

- Is information about the progress of the programme shared between the community and agency?

- Are the programme staff adequately qualified and experienced to carry out their jobs? If not, what kind of training could be organised to improve their competence?

- Does vehicle maintenance use up a lot of time and programme funds? Is there a better way of providing and managing programme transport?

Further reading

Boot, M.T. (1991), *Just Stir Gently: The way to mix hygiene education with water supply and sanitation*. Technical Paper Series 29, The Hague: IRC.

Feachem, R. and Cairncross, A.M. (1988), *Small Scale Sanitation*, London: Ross Institute.

Feachem, R. and Cairncross, A.M. (1978), *Small Water Supplies*, London: Ross Institute.

Flanagan, D. R. (1987), *Training Skills for Supervisors*. Training Series No.4, The Hague: IRC.

Franceys, R. with Pickford, J. and Reed, R. (1992), *A Guide to the Development of On-site Sanitation*, Geneva: WHO.

Jordan, T. D. (1984), *A Handbook of Gravity Flow Water Systems for Small Communities*. London: IT Publications.

Morgan P. (1990), *Rural Water Supplies and Sanitation*. Blair Research Bulletin, Basingstoke: Macmillan.

Watt, S.B. and Wood, W.E. (1979), *Hand Dug Wells and their Construction*, London: IT Publications.

Wegelin-Schuringa, M. (1991), *On-site Sanitation: Building on local practice*. Occasional Paper Series 16, The Hague: IRC.

Werner, D. and Bower, W (1982), *Helping Health Workers Learn: A book of methods, aids and ideas for instructors at the village level,* Palo Alto: Hesperian Foundation.

Managing community water supplies

Managing a community water supply successfully means operating and maintaining a system on a day-to-day basis so that it continues to work and supply water as planned. In its broadest sense, the management of a water supply also includes the promotion of the hygienic handling and use of water to improve the health of people in a community.

6.1 Management options

There are many different types of water system and they involve different types of management. A water system might be one handpump in a village or it might be a complex gravity system serving several thousand households. Whatever the size of the system there are three main ways in which community water supply systems can be managed:

- Agency managed: the agency, often a government water agency, constructs and manages a water supply on behalf of the users.

- Agency/community managed: the agency has a joint arrangement to manage a water supply with the community.

- Community managed: the community takes full responsibility for the management of its water supply.

Each of the above management options will now be examined more closely with reference to specific case studies.

Agency managed

Typically, agency managed supplies involve a government water agency which, in some countries, is the legal owner of all rural water supply schemes and is responsible for their management. Unfortunately, many government agencies have problems in managing water supplies successfully for the following reasons:

- A shortage of spare parts and tools can result in long breakdown times and in some cases the abandonment of equipment. This shortage is usually due to insufficient consideration by donors of long-term spare parts supply. There may be several factors involved:

  ◆ At the time of installation, donors did not include enough spare parts with initial equipment orders.

  ◆ A lack of local suppliers leads to difficulties in getting spare parts for equipment obtained from outside the country.

  ◆ A shortage of foreign exchange prevents government agencies from purchasing sufficient spare parts for imported equipment.

  ◆ A lack of standardisation results in many different types of equipment, from all over the world, being used in the same programme. It is usually an impossible task to stock enough spares for all the different models.

- A shortage of serviceable vehicles makes the support of operation and maintenance very difficult. This shortage is due to a number of factors:

  ◆ A shortage of spare parts and specialist tools as explained above.

  ◆ Donors are more inclined to supply vehicles for the implementation stage of a programme than for operation and maintenance.

  ◆ Maintenance work usually involves driving on poor roads, which damages vehicles.

  ◆ Vehicles for maintenance teams will not last long if the vehicles are inappropriate or not serviced well because of a lack of skilled mechanics and spare parts.

- A shortage of skills for both the repair and servicing of vehicles and equipment (such as pumps) hinders effective maintenance.

- Poor conditions of pay and employment in government service often mean that maintenance crews are unenthusiastic about field work.

In Ethiopia, for example, centralised management of rural water supplies has been common, and can give rise to problems:

The Water Supply and Sewerage Authority (WSSA) was legally responsible for managing all the water supply systems in the country outside the capital, Addis Ababa. In the case of a small rural handpump supply, handpump breakdowns were reported by the community to the local WSSA regional office, who should then dispatch a repair crew to repair the pump.

In reality, however, it might be several weeks before a maintenance crew arrived to repair the pump, for many of the reasons outlined above: a lack of spare parts, vehicles and maintenance crews.

In the case of some of the motorised pumped supplies in Ethiopia, however, the community has taken on certain of the management functions to try to overcome the problems of centralised management. This approach falls into the next category of water supply management.

Agency/community managed water supplies

In this case, the community plays an active role in managing the system but still does not own it. Major repair jobs and decisions affecting the future of the system are still in the hands of the agency who built it.

This type of management system was practised in the community of Dulecha, southern Ethiopia:

The water supply was a borehole and distribution system, managed by the community with the support of the water authority, WSSA. A water committee was formed with the help of WSSA extension agents and based on WSSA guidelines established for community management. A pump operator and a water point attendant were paid from funds collected from the sale of water. The water point attendant sold water at the standpost at a rate, or tariff, fixed by WSSA. The revenue was handed over to the treasurer of the water committee. The treasurer and chairman were responsible for buying diesel for the pump and for paying the two employees.

This method of running the system at a community level reduced the operational burden on the water authority and passed some control to a water committee. But what happened if the system broke down?

Under an agreement between WSSA and the community, 40 per cent of all profits from the sale of water was intended to go into a maintenance fund. In practice this seldom happened because the

143

systems showed only a marginal profit, due to the low tariff and the high cost of diesel.

Tariffs need to be set at a realistic level if sufficient funds are to be generated to cover maintenance costs. However, fixing a tariff is not straightforward, as will be considered later. In the Dulecha example, the water committee managed the day-to-day running of the system. Major repairs remained the responsibility of WSSA who still legally owned the system.

Community managed water supplies

In the case of a truly community managed water supply, the members of the community actually own, operate and maintain the supply. The question of ownership is central to true community management.

The Murugi-Mugomango Water Society in the Meru District of Kenya provides an example of a community managed water supply. The Society developed from small self-help groups, and relied upon advice and support from a variety of external agencies:

The Murugi-Mugomango Water Society grew out of the amalgamation of seven small self-help groups in 1983. In 1984 the Society signed an agreement with an NGO, who agreed to give financial support to the Society in the extension of a gravity-fed water distribution system to yard connections supplying 2,000 families. The Society members were inexperienced in management and financial accounting, and they lacked the ability to mobilise their communities beyond the initial fund-raising activities. They obtained training and technical assistance from a Kenya-based international NGO, and a Kenyan consulting firm.

The Society originally raised funds by establishing a membership subscription. People who wanted a yard connection paid the subscription and agreed to provide 60 days' labour for construction. Institutions, like schools and clinics, who also wanted a supply paid a higher subscription fee. By August 1991 there were 2,141 members, of whom 1,340 had received a yard connection, through 310km of pipelines.

In this example, funds for the development of the water supply were raised from within the community through the system of subscriptions. For some members a subscription was relatively expensive, and had to be paid in small instalments. Only then were they entitled to a yard connection. In this way a form of saving for a connection was encouraged. But what about the long-term operation and maintenance of the supply?

All house connections were metered. Members paid a water tariff of Ksh20 (US$0.70) per 30 cubic metres per month. If they used more, they had to pay an additional Ksh2 for every extra cubic metre.

There were very few people who did not pay their water bills. The tariff was set at a level people could afford and were willing to pay. The relatively large quantity of water that was available at a fixed rate meant that people used the water for small gardens. There was therefore a strong economic incentive to support the efficient management of the supply:

The Society had its own constitution and was run in a very business-like manner, with the objective of making a small profit. A management committee was elected every two years. During the construction phase, the international NGO held training courses for the management committee in subjects such as financial accounting, record keeping, planning and management.

The water users had a say in the running of the water supply through the elected management committee. Committee members were held accountable, and could be replaced at the next election if members were unhappy with their performance.

The Society directly employed a project manager and skilled staff, including an accountant, cashier, secretary, technical supervisors, plumbers and storekeepers. The staff were accountable to the project manager, and the manager was accountable to the management committee.

It was obviously in the interests of the staff to carry out their tasks competently, for their jobs depended on the efficient running of the supply. This is in contrast to government employees in a water authority who may have no direct interest in the operation and maintenance of a supply.

The Water Department of the Government of Kenya has supported the Society by providing technical advice during construction and funding for the office buildings and store, but has no direct involvement in the management of the supply.

The Murugi-Mugumango Water Society has been successful in the context of Meru District, Kenya, but applying the approach to other programmes would need care. The Society's supply was from a reliable, clear mountain stream which required little treatment and could be distributed by gravity. Such a convenient supply would not necessarily be available elsewhere. However, there are still important features of the scheme which are of relevance to other programmes:

- The demand for an improved water supply scheme came from the people.

- Procedures for managing the system were developed by the community with external specialist support.

- There were NGOs who were prepared to support the local initiative with inputs the Society lacked: funds, technical assistance and training.

- A spirit of self-help already existed in the community, and people were familiar with the workings of a society from their experience in the agricultural sector.

- Members of the Society made significant contributions of money and labour, which helped to create a strong sense of ownership of the system.

- The Government of Kenya have provided the legal framework for the establishment of community societies to manage their own affairs.

- The level of literacy and numeracy in the community, the availability of banking facilities, and a strong local cash economy allowed the application of a business approach to water management. The Society operates on a commercial basis, employing qualified staff. The scheme does not rely on volunteers, as many other water schemes are expected to do.

- The water was supplied to yard connections. This meant the water points were not communally owned but owned and cared for by each household. Private connections are usually easier to manage than communal water points.

- There was a good supply of water, which was used for small-scale irrigation of gardens and in crop processing, like coffee washing. There was therefore an economic incentive to manage the water supply efficiently.

The above conditions would not all be met in many other situations, especially in remote rural areas where the cash economy has not been well developed. Nevertheless, the case provides useful lessons which could be of value to other programmes.

6.2 Community management

Several different aspects of community management will now be looked at more closely.

Ownership and responsibility for a water supply

There needs to be a clear understanding of community responsibilities for a water supply if it is to be used and looked after effectively:

In an Ethiopian dug-wells programme a covered access opening had been provided in the cover-slab of a well so that if the handpump broke down the community could still collect water by bucket and rope. The cover over the opening was sealed to the slab with cement so as to prevent waste water entering the well from spilt handpump water. In one particular case when the handpump failed to work, however, nobody in the community felt they had the responsibility to break the cement seal to lift the cover off. The well remained unused for a considerable period of time until the agency was able to repair the handpump.

It was felt that the well was owned by the agency and not by the community. There was a need to encourage community responsibility for the well. The community needed guidance and lacked the confidence to deal with even minor operational problems.

Contributions from individual members of a community may be important in developing a sense of community ownership and responsibility. Contributions are usually in the form of labour or money.

Contributions of labour

Contributing labour is sometimes a requirement before a household can get a water supply:

Under the constitution of the Murugi-Mugomango Society, members dug their own household service pipe trench leading from the main pipeline. It was felt that contributing time and effort in this way would increase members' sense of responsibility towards the supply and would lead to a greater sense of commitment to keeping the system operating in the future.

Contributions of money

A system of community cash contributions towards the cost of running a water system is becoming more common, particularly in areas where a strong cash economy exists:

In the Wenchi district of northern Ghana, a mission water programme asked communities to contribute 70,000 cedis (US$300) towards the cost of a borehole and handpump. There were acute water shortages during the dry season. The mission had no difficulty collecting this money, part of which was paid in to a maintenance fund. As maintenance was carried out and paid for, communities made further payments into the fund.

Community contributions to maintenance funds are an essential requirement for community management of water supplies.

Water committees

The formation of water committees has often been proposed in the past as an effective way of managing a water supply:

The job of extension agents in the Ethiopian Water Supply and Sewerage Authority (WSSA) Community Participation Service was to form water committees at all new construction sites. WSSA guidelines stated that water committees should comprise five to seven people, at least two of whom should be women. The extension agents also had a list of officers, with job descriptions, who were to be on each committee.

Some of the water committees with responsibility for motorised pumped supplies functioned efficiently, as in the case of Dulecha described previously. But the water committees for most handpump installations did not function as intended, and seldom met after being formed. There were several reasons for this:

* The role of a water committee was not made clear.

* For a handpump supply, there was not much for a committee to do on a regular basis.

* Handpump caretakers were not supplied with tools, so they could not repair handpumps; and this undermined the committee's role.

* Each committee saw the handpump as belonging to the government. There was no sense of ownership or responsibility for the handpump.

* Water committees had no real authority to act within the community.

* Power in each community was held by a political committee.

In places where the water committee did function, the following characteristics were common:

- Members of the water committee were also members of the political committee.

- The committee members were regularly active because they had things to do, such as the collection of water charges, the purchase of fuel for the pump, and the employment and supervision of a pump operator and a waterpoint attendant.

- When it was found that WSSA could not provide spare parts for the water system, the committee purchased the parts.

Before forming a water committee it is important to be clear about what the committee should do and whether a committee is really necessary. Existing community management structures should be considered, as alternatives to a water committee.

In some cases there can be too many committees:

In Ethiopia during the 1980s, villages often had up to 12 committees: a development committee, a health committee, a water committee, a youth committee, a committee to run the community shop, a committee to run the Producers' Cooperative, a sports committee and so on.

Do communities need all these committees? It is often the case that the same people are on all the committees. This could be for a variety of reasons: because there are only so many competent people, because community and political leaders want to maintain control, or because only certain people are keen to volunteer.

It may be better for existing local organisations to take on the role of managing a water scheme rather than establish yet another committee:

In Ethiopia, water committees were formed through the local association, the kebele, which was a political structure. The water committee chairman was often the chairman of the kebele, which gave the water committee authority to act within the community.

But should a water committee be based on a local political structure or should it try to be separate? These structures may not always represent all the people in a community fairly. However, if local political structures are bypassed, then members of a water committee may not have the authority to carry out their tasks.

Where traditional structures are still strong they should be respected:

During the Water Utilisation Project in the Upper Regions of Ghana, the Ghana Water and Sewerage Corporation (GWSC) would always approach the village chief to suggest the formation of a water committee. GWSC then had the backing of the most influential person in the community. The chief often became chairman of the water committee, so the committee had the authority to take and implement decisions.

However, committees do not always have the support of the people. The representation of individuals in a community was considered in Chapter 2. The point was made that traditional structures may exclude certain members of the community, especially women, who have an interest in the management of a water supply. Modifications to traditional practice may need to be encouraged in these circumstances.

Community agreements

In some cases, it may be advisable for a community and agency to enter into a formal written agreement about the roles and responsibilities of each partner. In some countries such agreements are now required by the government agency responsible for water, if a community is to manage its own supply.

The aim of an agreement is to avoid misunderstandings between an agency and a community in the future management of a supply:

In southern Ethiopia the Water Supply and Sewerage Authority (WSSA) has a 'WSSA-Community Agreement' which spells out in detail the roles and responsibilities of both partners for every stage of the project cycle leading to the community management of a supply. The Agreement is explained to village leaders at an early stage, and representatives of both WSSA and the community sign the Agreement before construction starts.

An agreement often covers the complete project cycle from planning to management, and can include the following points:

The responsibilities of the water committee, on behalf of the community:

- Decide, with agency technical advice, on the most appropriate water source and how to protect it.

- Participate in the planning of the improved water supply.

- Decide on the best time to start construction.

- Organise voluntary or paid community labour for construction.

- Organise contributions of local construction materials.

- Recruit and employ caretakers and waterpoint attendants.

- Establish charges for water, collect payments regularly and keep financial accounts.

- Purchase spare parts when necessary.

- Report major breakdowns to the water agency.

- Keep accurate records of the water system.

- Encourage people to use the improved water supply.

- Promote hygienic water use practices.

- Promote good sanitation practices.

The responsibilities of the agency:

- Draw up an agreement with the community.

- Carry out a preliminary survey.

- Prepare a project report and site plan.

- Assist in the formation of a water committee if appropriate.

- Provide skilled staff and non-local materials.

- Provide transport for workers and materials.

- Provide finance for construction.

- Train members of the water committee in management skills.

- Train caretakers and waterpoint attendants.

- Supply a basic tool kit for caretakers.

- Supervise the construction and maintenance work.

- Carry out major maintenance and repair work if the community are only able to take responsibility for minor maintenance.

- Supply spare parts at cost to the water committee.

- Monitor community management and offer advice as needed.

Agencies should be sensitive to the need to avoid complicated and lengthy agreements. An agreement should be in a form which can be clearly understood by the water committee and members of the community.

One way to ensure understanding is for the agreement to be drawn up with the active participation of the community. However, in practice, agreements are often standardised.

The advantages of a standard agreement are that it avoids the situation where one community has a more advantageous agreement than a neighbouring community. For example, all communities should pay the same contributions for major maintenance carried out by the water agency. It is also more convenient for a government water agency, who would find it confusing if they had different agreements with each community.

In several countries, including Ghana and Ethiopia, there are national guidelines for the drawing up of community-agency agreements. Scope for local agreements may then be restricted. The best approach, and the extent to which standard agreements can be adapted to local circumstances, will depend on government policy and the situation in each country.

For each community-agency agreement, time needs to be allowed for consultation both within the community and between the agency and community representatives. This process may slow down the rate of construction in a programme but is well worth the effort in the long term if an agreement leads to a clear understanding of each partner's responsibilities. Time should be allowed for adequate consultation in programme planning. Donors should be made aware of the need to spend time on this activity to avoid unrealistic, donor imposed targets which concentrate only on construction.

Training

Agencies have an important part to play in the training of community members in operation, maintenance and management skills. Management training can include the following:

- Administrative training including the keeping of records.

- Keeping accounts — recording revenue and expenditure.

- Spare parts management.

- Managing the operation and maintenance of the system

    — employing and training staff

— providing tools and equipment

— spare parts supply.

- The organisation of hygiene education.

- Planning for the future expansion of the system.

The training of caretakers and management committee members is best carried out within the community:

An NGO used to train community handpump caretakers during a two-week course at the regional water authority workshop compound in Awassa, Ethiopia. Communities had to provide an allowance for their trainees' accommodation and food while they were away from the village.

This approach involved the community in finding the funds to send the trainees to the district town. It also accidentally excluded most women from being handpump caretakers, as it was culturally unacceptable for them to be away from their house overnight without their husbands, especially in a town:

The NGO modified its approach, and brought the trainers to the trainees in the villages. Women extension staff replaced workshop-based technicians as the trainers.

This approach made it more convenient for people to attend and encouraged more women to become handpump caretakers. A review of the training after six months made two main comments:

- The training of trainees only during the installation period was inadequate. There needed to be further follow-up, with more training sessions organised on site.

- The training of trainers needed to be improved. Often, the trainers found it difficult to step back and allow the trainee caretakers to practice what they had learnt.

The training of committee members can also be held in the community:

At Murugi-Mugomango, management training took place in the offices of the Water Society. In southern Ethiopia, the training of management committee members took place at the house of a committee member or at the local administration office.

If training is carried out locally, this enables committee members to attend without the difficulties of travelling, and women members to attend who would find it difficult to do so otherwise. Trainees feel more comfortable in familiar surroundings.

Wolayta, Ethiopia. Training on site allows more women to become handpump caretakers.

There need to be enough trainers available to train water committee members:

In southern Ethiopia, the government water agency is developing training courses on the management of community water systems for extension workers from NGOs operating in the region. The NGO extension workers will then conduct management training sessions with water committees at sites where new water systems are to be constructed.

The joint involvement of several agencies in the training of water committees ensures a uniform approach within the same locality.

One of the first jobs of the water committee might be to appoint a caretaker or a pump operator.

154

Caretakers and operators

Caretakers and operators will be required to carry out day-to-day operation and maintenance duties. They may be employed by the community through the water committee or have some other arrangement, such as payment in kind for the work they do. Criteria were established in southern Ethiopia to assist water committees in the selection of handpump caretakers. A caretaker should preferably:

- Be a long-time resident.
- Be a respected member of the community.
- Live close to the handpump.
- Have had some mechanical experience, such as repairing bicycles or operating a grinding mill.
- Be prepared to volunteer or receive a small allowance, depending on the local community arrangement.
- Be prepared to attend training.

The typical duties of a handpump caretaker included:

- Daily inspection of the pump and well surroundings.
- Preventive maintenance tasks.
- Reporting of major breakdowns to the water committee.
- Monitoring of the well yield.

In the past, agencies have promoted the idea of voluntary caretakers. But expecting people to do responsible, semi-skilled work on a voluntary basis in communities which are struggling economically is often unrealistic. Communities should be encouraged to give some incentive to handpump caretakers:

Village water committees in Damot Gale district of Wolayta, Ethiopia, pay a small allowance to handpump caretakers from the money collected from the monthly water charges.

If a community is to manage a water supply system, the technology used needs to be of a type that community caretakers can maintain with little outside assistance:

An NGO installed a handpump on a hand-dug well in Lamarada, Ethiopia. Two women caretakers were taught how to install the handpump, and some maintenance procedures. The caretakers practised the procedure of removing the pump rods to replace the rubber seal and the rubber bobbin on the plunger assembly. They were also taught how to replace the plastic bushes which support the fulcrum pin and the hanger pin. A spare parts kit was given to the water committee at the time of installation.

The caretakers can now carry out regular maintenance and minor repairs on the pump without outside assistance. This is an example of a technology which is appropriate for community management. It is often referred to as a Village Level Operation and Maintenance (VLOM) technology for this reason.

There may be situations where a handpump breakdown is beyond the ability of the caretaker to repair, and agency support will be needed:

The handle of a village handpump broke one day. The caretaker had neither the equipment, nor the skill to repair it. Through the water committee she sent a message to the support agency requesting either a new handle or a maintenance crew to come and weld the broken handle.

It does not usually make financial or technical sense to provide every handpump caretaker with a full tool kit and training to carry out non-routine maintenance and repair work. This kind of work can be done by a water agency under a community-agency agreement. In many cases, however, the time between breakdown and repair can still be several weeks — or even months — despite the obligations of an agreement.

An alternative to reliance on a government water agency is for the community, through the water committee, to contract major repair work to the private sector. Agencies can promote private sector services by providing pump maintenance training to local mechanics. Larger bilateral, multilateral and government agencies need to consider the possibility of supplying spare parts to private mechanics through private commercial traders.

Most handpumps have a simple maintenance manual but these are often in English or French, not a local language. If caretakers can read their own language, then training material, and operation and maintenance guides, should be translated into the local language:

In Ethiopia, the Water Supply and Sewerage Authority translated a handpump maintenance card from English into Amharic. The British manufacturer of the pump was then asked to print the Amharic version on plasticised cards. These cards are now given to each handpump caretaker after training.

One problem with translation is that there may be no words in a local language for technical terms:

> *Part of a handpump training course in northern Ghana involved trainees in the identification of words in their own language, Mampruli, to represent technical terms for which there was no equivalent Mampruli word. Parts of the body were used to represent the parts of a handpump. The outlet was called 'the mouth'; the base was called 'the foot'; the handle was called 'the arm', and so on.*

Extension staff need to ensure that any material which is given to caretakers and water committee members can be readily understood.

Hygiene education

Caretakers may take responsibility for basic hygiene education at the waterpoint so that in the course of their operation and maintenance work they can also encourage the hygienic handling of water.

More organised hygiene education should be arranged through the management committee to continue the hygiene education work carried out during the development of the supply. For this to happen effectively, links may need to be established between the management committee, community health services, and village health workers. The agency can have an important role in making these links to promote the continuation of hygiene education well beyond the construction stage of an improved water supply.

6.3 Financing operation and maintenance

Charging for water

The operation, maintenance and management of a water supply costs money. This is true whether it is agency managed or community managed. The money for the running of a supply must come from somewhere. If dependence on outside support is to be reduced to a minimum, the users must contribute financially to the management of their own supply.

The method of charging for the upkeep of a water supply will depend upon how often operation and maintenance costs will need to be covered and on the level of costs involved:

> *The maintenance of an open well in northern Ghana entailed the replacement of buckets and ropes as they wore out. This was the*

responsibility of each village. The average cost of replacement was estimated at 3,000 cedis ($9) per well per year. Regular charges for water were inappropriate in this case, because the costs could be covered by a household collection whenever the buckets and ropes needed replacing.

The cost of water supply maintenance can vary from the regular replacement of a worn out bucket to the major replacement of broken pipes. Household collections at the time of a breakdown may raise insufficient funds for repairs if the costs are high. In this case, regular charges may be necessary to build up a maintenance fund.

In some countries the regular water charge, or tariff, is set by the government water agency, as in Ethiopia. In other countries the tariff is set by each community, as in Kenya.

There are three important considerations in setting a water tariff: it should be affordable to the users; they must be willing to pay; and there must be a system of penalties for not paying.

The following case study from northern Ghana illustrates the way in which a water tariff may be introduced and implemented. It should be noted that this tariff was introduced for handpumps which had already been installed, without any prior arrangement with communities for long-term maintenance payments. Therefore, it was a big change to ask people to pay for water which had previously been supplied free:

A rural water tariff was introduced by Ghana Water and Sewerage Corporation (GWSC) in 1986. It was explained to the 2,600 communities in the Upper Regions which had a handpump that a tariff was being introduced to offset the cost of spare parts for pumps and maintenance vehicles, and to help to pay the wages of maintenance staff. It was also explained that the tariff was not for the sale of water, which was God-given and therefore free, but was to help to cover the cost of obtaining safe drinking water. Each community was informed about ways of paying the tariff and the penalties for late or non-payment.

Village water committees decided how the tariff would be collected. In the first year, about 75 per cent of the communities paid initially, but after follow-up of non-payers, nearly all the communities eventually paid. The tariff was increased gradually each year, and collection rates were 85 per cent and 86 per cent for the second and third years. It was made easier for communities to pay the tariff by sending accounting personnel to local markets to collect the money and issue receipts. Reductions were also offered if communities paid early.

The introduction of a tariff on handpumps was judged to have been a success in the Upper Regions of Ghana for the following reasons:

- It was affordable.

- Most households were willing to pay the level of tariff introduced.

- Most households recognised the benefits of having access to a safe water supply.

- An effective education campaign was conducted at the outset to explain the reasons for payment.

- The arrangements for payment were made convenient for the communities.

- GWSC maintenance crews were able to keep an average of 95 per cent of handpumps working and therefore there was an incentive to pay.

The only communities who did not pay were those with a reliable alternative source closer than the handpumps.

Despite the efforts made in the Upper Regions programme, the charges were still not economic. That is, the cost of handpump maintenance continued to be subsidised, because the charges did not cover the full costs. The maintenance of the handpumps was also carried out by GWSC maintenance crews, not by the villagers themselves. This arrangement meant that, for GWSC, rural handpump maintenance was still a considerable burden which could not be easily sustained. For the communities, it meant that they were still dependent on external maintenance support which could not be guaranteed.

A later programme attempted to overcome these problems by transferring more of the responsibility for handpump maintenance to the community:

In 1991, a water programme in the Gambaga district of northern Ghana installed Afridev handpumps on boreholes for village water supplies. Villages paid an initial contribution of 80,000 cedis ($242) towards the cost of each handpump and concrete pad. The agency then advised villages on how much they should aim to collect to cover the cost of regular maintenance. This was estimated at 70,000 cedis ($212) per year. Therefore, for an average number of 300 pump users, the charge worked out at an acceptable 20 cedis ($0.06) per person per month. Two village handpump caretakers were trained for each handpump, and village water committees were established to manage the supplies.

In this case, the villages were advised to collect money on a regular basis to build up a fund to cover the maintenance and replacement costs of each pump installed. It was then the responsibility of each village to maintain its pump and only call upon the government water agency for major repairs, which were to be paid for by the village.

Financial management

Community management of a water supply involves the collection and keeping of money. Experience shows that, in order to avoid corruption and misappropriation of funds, there needs to be some system of safeguarding the money. This is made simpler if there are rural banks within easy reach of communities. However, in rural northern Ghana and Ethiopia, for example, this is not the case.

Where there are no banking facilities, government agencies may assist water committees by collecting the funds and banking them in the name of the community, as happened in the Upper Regions of Ghana. Where alternative arrangements cannot be made, water committees have to keep money in their homes. This can present a big temptation to use the money for other things, especially in times of need.

The training of water committee members can help to overcome some of the problems in the handling of money for community maintenance:

Revenue staff from the Water Supply and Sewerage Authority in Awassa, Ethiopia, met with each water committee chairman and treasurer at the site of the motorised pumped schemes for which the committee members were responsible. The committee members were shown how to complete accounts detailing the income from water sales and expenses, such as diesel and salaries, and how to produce a balance sheet. Several visits were necessary to complete the training.

The money left over after the payment of expenses was used by the committees to buy spare parts from the water authority when serious breakdowns occurred.

Community confidence, knowledge and skills can be built up during the development of a supply so that community management can follow. A community's ability to manage a supply will depend to a great extent on the level of its involvement during the development of the supply.

Checklist of questions

In the programme in which you are involved:

- What kind of management system will be left in place?

- Can water supplies be kept working in the long term under the present management system?

- Who owns the completed water supplies?

- Who is responsible for the operation and maintenance of the water supplies?

- Are water committees the best way to organise the community management of water supplies or are there alternative community structures which could do this job better?

- Who is going to draw up the community-agency agreement?

- Is management training provided for members of the community?

- Where does the money come from for operation and maintenance?

- Should water users be charged more for their water to cover the costs of operation and maintenance and if so, how will people respond?

- Do communities have full control of the money collected for the management of their water supplies?

Further reading

Bastmeyer, T. and Visscher, J.T. (1987), *Maintenance Systems for Rural Water Supplies*. Occasional Paper Series No.8, The Hague: IRC.

Evans, P. (1992), *Paying the Piper*. Occasional Paper Series No.18, The Hague: IRC.

IRC, (1991), *Piped Supplies for Small Communities: Applying the partnership approach*, The Hague: IRC.

McCommon, C.; Warner, D.; Johalem, D.; (1990), *Community Management of Rural Water Supply and Sanitation Services*. Technical Report No.67, Arlington, VA: WASH.

Wijk-Sijbesma, C. (1989), *What Price Water? User participation in paying for community based water supply (with particular emphasis on piped systems)*. Occasional Paper Series No.10, The Hague: IRC.

7

Evaluation for planning

The process of evaluation aims to determine the impact of a programme by reference to the original objectives:

- Have the original programme objectives been achieved?
- If the objectives have not been achieved, why not?
- What has been achieved instead?

An evaluation draws on information from the following sources:

- Baseline information gathered during the planning stage.
- Information from programme monitoring.
- Information collected at the time of the evaluation.

By drawing on these sources of information, the situation before and after the implementation of a programme's activities can be compared. It is then possible to see if the programme's aims and objectives have been achieved.

An evaluation will not just be concerned with factual data such as the number of wells dug or of pumps working. It will also be concerned with the community's ability to manage and effectively use its improved water supply and sanitation facilities.

A mid-term evaluation normally assesses a programme's progress half-way through its planned duration. In practice, however, an evaluation could take place at any time from the start of a programme to several years after completion of the implementation stage.

The lessons learned from a programme may be of use to other programmes. An evaluation, therefore, not only assesses whether objectives have been met, but also includes recommendations for the planning of future programmes. Hence the title of this chapter: *evaluation for planning*.

Some programme staff may feel uneasy about an evaluation because they might assume that their work performance is under investigation. This is not the intention of an evaluation and it is important to make this clear to staff. They should be briefed on the aims of the evaluation and how they can participate by contributing their ideas on the programme's progress and future.

7.1 Internal evaluations

An internal evaluation is an evaluation carried out by the partners in a programme — the agency and community — without outside assistance.

In a wells programme in northern Ghana a system of internal evaluations, or reviews, was followed:

Village and agency representatives took part in annual review meetings. These took place following harvesting, at the beginning of each new construction season. At this time, some villages would be thinking of improving their water supplies, while others would have gained some experience from previously improved supplies. The aim was to evaluate the progress of the programme from those directly involved so that past experience could help in the planning of new projects.

Such reviews require understanding and co-operation between partners if evaluations are to be effective. The aim is to obtain critical feedback from the people directly affected by a programme. The agency must be willing and able to accept criticism and respond in a constructive way. To continue the case above:

In the first joint review meeting, questions were asked by the village representatives concerning the length of the planned programme: 'What was the basis for setting this three-year programme? Will all the wells be finished in all the villages in this time or does it mean you only have enough money for three years' work?'

A lot of discussion followed and it was concluded that it was not possible to complete the work in all the villages in the allocated time. The agency had set the time of the programme according to the available funds but had not involved the community in making this decision. This made the agency representatives realise how little the community had been involved in major decisions concerning the programme. The evaluation led to the greater involvement of the community, through the establishment of a water committee to represent the villages involved:

> *The committee took over responsibility for assessing the requests from villages for assistance and the drawing up of a schedule of well construction. The committee then advised the agency on the timescale of a realistic programme to serve all the interested villages.*

For an evaluation to be effective, its recommendations need to be put into practice.

Damot Gale, Ethiopia. Water committee members can monitor and evaluate the performance of their own water supplies.

Pilot demonstration programmes require evaluation on completion. The purpose is to assess the approach before developing a larger-scale programme:

> *An evaluation workshop was held at the end of a four-month well-digging pilot training programme in Gambaga, northern Ghana. The workshop included trainers, trainees, and village representatives. The*

aim was to learn from everyone's experience in order to produce a proposal for a larger programme.

Various issues were identified. They included technical matters such as improvements in safety and reporting procedures, and further trials on well-lining techniques. Important feedback came from the community representatives concerning organisation at the village level:

The representatives felt each community needed more time to consider the financial and management aspects of digging its own wells, compared to an alternative, borehole supply. The community representatives also felt they had been asked to carry too much responsibility, and requested further support from the extension agents.

The results of the evaluation workshop were agreed by the participants and recorded in an evaluation report. The evaluation report was used as a reference in drawing up a proposal for a future programme. This kind of feedback from a pilot programme is essential if a follow-up programme is to incorporate the experience of both agency staff and community members.

7.2 External and joint evaluations

External evaluations are carried out by evaluators who are neither members of the community nor on the staff of the agency. External evaluators are independent and therefore it is hoped they will provide a more objective view of a programme than internal evaluators. External evaluators with a good background knowledge of a programme are often able to see the broader issues more clearly than someone who has been closely involved on a day-to-day basis.

A funding agency carried out an evaluation of a long-term rural water programme they had been funding in Gama Gofa, Ethiopia:

The funding agency contracted a consultant to coordinate an external evaluation. Technical information was gathered over a period of three months prior to the core evaluation period. The technical surveys were carried out by a local NGO water team with experience of this kind of work. A local sociologist was contracted to obtain information concerning life style, practices, and opinions, which would have been difficult to gather unless the researcher spoke the language and knew the customs of the community.

The combination of sociological and technical skills enabled essential information to be collected on which to base the evaluation. It is significant that, owing to the lack of substantial monitoring during the implementation stage of the programme, a considerable preliminary period for gathering information was required. This would not have been necessary if monitoring had been carried out as a planned activity from the beginning of the programme.

The disadvantages of an external evaluation are:

- There is a lack of detailed programme knowledge within the evaluation team.

- External evaluators are usually short of time and so they are not able to visit many project sites.

- An external approach is less likely to encourage self-evaluation by programme staff and community members.

It is preferable, therefore, for external evaluators to adopt a joint evaluation approach in which staff and members of the community also have an opportunity to contribute to the evaluation. To continue the previous case:

Although the funding agency had contracted an outside consultant to co-ordinate the evaluation, the agency was also keen for the programme staff to be involved. Regular meetings were arranged with staff to discuss the findings as the evaluation proceeded. Misunderstandings on the part of the evaluation team could then be corrected and information clarified. The exercise helped staff to reflect on their own activities, using the observations made by the external evaluators. It was hoped that this experience would be useful for staff in future monitoring and evaluation.

It is regrettable that, in practice, many external evaluations do not allow enough time for substantial community involvement in the evaluation process. This could be overcome if more time were allowed for evaluations than has been customary in the past. Just as agency staff can be involved through regular meetings and discussions during an evaluation, so also could community members and representatives.

Joint evaluations can involve a wide range of people, from government agencies to external consultants:

A four-week evaluation was initiated by two agencies who, together, had a substantial water programme covering a large geographical area. The evaluation terms of reference stipulated a team of six members. Four members were external consultants: team leader, sociologist, economist and engineer. The other two members were representatives of the government water agency and the Ministry of Health. The evaluation procedure called for end-of-week meetings between the evaluators and programme staff. The meetings provided feedback and comment on the progress and content of the evaluation.

This type of joint evaluation had the advantage of involving a broad range of people as practically as possible. It combined the relative advantages of outside independence and internal knowledge. The involvement of government representatives provided guidance on government policy and strategies in the water sector.

The regular feedback and opportunities for comment ensured that the results of the final evaluation report were not unexpected. It is important that it is well known and understood how the recommendations were arrived at. Acceptance of the evaluation recommendations is then more likely.

The sharing of evaluation results, both successes and failures, helps in the process of learning from each other's practical experience. The sharing of experience should be encouraged to guide the planning of future programmes.

Checklist of questions

- Has an evaluation been planned for your programme?

- What are the main areas of concern in your programme that should be included in an evaluation?

- Would the programme staff and members of the community be willing and able to work together in a joint evaluation of your programme?

- Would programme staff feel threatened by an evaluation and if so, what can be done about this?

- How can the community be involved in the evaluation process?

Further reading

Boot, M.T. and Cairncross, S. (editors) (1993), *Actions Speak: The study of hygiene behaviour in water supply and sanitation projects*, The Hague: IRC and London School of Hygiene and Tropical Medicine.

Caincross S., Carruthers I., Curtis D., Feachem R., Bradley D., Baldwin G. (1980), *Evaluation for Village Water Supply Planning*, Technical Paper Series No.15, The Hague: IRC International Water and Sanitation Centre.

Feuerstein, M.T. (1987), *Partners in Evaluation: Evaluating development and community programmes with participants*, Basingstoke: Macmillan.

WHO (1983), *Minimum Evaluation Procedure (MEP) for Water Supply and Sanitation Projects*, Geneva: WHO.

Appendix 1

Microbiological water quality

It is not practical to test for all the harmful organisms that might be present in water. However, the majority of water quality problems in rural supplies are related to organisms originating in human excreta. The faecal coliform bacteria, *E. Coli*, are always present in human excreta and therefore they are used as an indicator of contamination.

It is important to remember that *E. Coli* bacteria may not be harmful in themselves but their presence indicates that there may be other organisms in the water which could be harmful. Generally, the higher the number of *E. Coli* bacteria present, the higher the risk of the water causing illness.

The standard form of referring to the number of *E. Coli* bacteria in water is the number of *E. Coli* bacteria present in a 100ml sample of the water under test: *E. Coli*/100ml.

Microbiological guidelines and standards

The WHO guidelines for safe drinking water say there should be no faecal coliforms present in water if it is to be fit for drinking. This is therefore expressed as 0 *E. Coli*/100ml. However, many people consider this too strict.

The danger of setting a standard of 0 *E. Coli*/100ml is that many existing supplies would not meet the standard and therefore they would be closed down. This action would leave the even more polluted, unprotected sources as the only alternative water supplies and would therefore create an even greater health risk.

In the foreseeable future, it would not be economically or technically feasible to bring all water supplies up to the desired water quality standard of 0 *E. Coli*/100ml. Therefore, in practice, less strict figures are often accepted, although the desired aim is still to achieve 0 *E. Coli*/100ml, if possible. In some countries, the figure used for a safe drinking water supply in rural areas is 10 *E. Coli*/100ml.

It must be remembered that the number of faecal coliform bacteria in water is only an *indicator* of water contamination and the 'WHO guidelines' are only *guidelines*, not standards. Each country, however, will have its own approach to water quality and may have established standards with which drinking water must comply.

Appendix 2

Sources of further information

The publications listed at the end of each chapter may be obtained from the following addresses:

IT Publications:
IT Publications
103-105 Southampton Row
London
WC1B 4HH
United Kingdom

IRC Publications:
IRC
International Water & Sanitation Centre
P.O. Box 93190
2509 AD The Hague
The Netherlands

Oxfam Publications:
Oxfam Publications
274 Banbury Road
Oxford
OX2 7DZ
United Kingdom

UNDP Publications:
UNDP
Division of Information
One UN Plaza
New York NY 10017
USA

WASH Publications:
WASH Operations Centre
1611 N. Kent St., Room 1001
Arlington, VA 22209
USA

WHO Publications:
WHO
Distribution and Sales Service
Avenue Appia
1211 Geneva 27
Switzerland

Publications referred to under 'Further Reading' for which there is no specific address listed may be available from the ITDG bookshop at the IT Publications address above.

Index